Whitie
The Cat
Who Rescued Humans

Mabel Elizabeth (Beth) Livingston

DEDICATION

This book is dedicated to my husband, Kurt. His unconditional love, support and most of all his dedication to our furry friends is my inspiration. Secondly, I want to dedicate this to Whitie. One of the best cats we ever had the privilege of loving. He truly was our King of the house. We miss him dearly but are comforted with the knowledge that he is exploring and will be waiting for us on the other side of the Rainbow Bridge where he will once again be our Whitie Cat.

ACKNOWLEDGMENTS

I want to thank the following people for their help with this book: Dr. Theresa Crater, my professor at SNHU, who helped guide me in my writing career as well as enabled me to create the character of Whitie

Tamalyn Scott Whitehead, author, friend, and encourager. She has shown me through the years that I can become an author as well as her guidance and support for this first of many novels.

Debra Blanchard, who was willing to take in our array of cats and give them a place to live when a house fire took our feet out from under us. I don't know of anyone else who would so willingly open their home to so many.

Barbara Rose, my closest friend, collogue, and encourager. You were there for me so many times when I wanted to give up and doubt my ability to write this. Without you, I would not have been held accountable.

Lastly, to all of my forever friends, both feline and canine. My pets have taught me the value of life and love. They have instilled in me the ability to love unconditionally and to cherish each one.

To all those animals who have come and gone and will continue to be welcomed into our home this is for you.

<<< **ONE** >>>

While humans assume that cats do not have stories to tell, I can assure you that I do. My story starts with a plastic box and the repugnant scent of death. Of course, my life was not always filled with death; but when death did make its ultimate appearance, there was, as it should be, an eternal earthly end. Not exactly the nine lives, as some humans imagine cats have, when in fact, we only have one. While I filled my humans' lives with excitement, they in turn, endeavored to make that single life for me one in which there was plenty of love, attention, and most of all the opportunity to rescue them. You might think that humans rescue cats, and that may be true, but cats are the ones who often rescue humans from their insanely hectic lives. So, it is a win-win situation for both of us. In my case though there was more than just myself, who came to this place of comfort, this house of welcoming those who were weary, hurt, and most of all in need of love. While at the same time not only was I being rescued but so were many of my feline friends. Let me begin my story at the beginning; as most stories obviously start.

I entered my home as an impetuous, yet amusing kitten along with my two siblings. My oldest and most aggressive littermate was a solid gray feline with emerald green eyes that often appeared to be gazing off into the future. Looking back on my sister now, perhaps the future was visible to her, due to the fact it was not that far off. My other littermate, another sister of course, had sparkling black eyes and long black fur, which always seemed to be needing constant attention. I began to grow weary of her forever licking, licking until she would hack up a hairball and just leave it lying on the floor. When that happened, we three always made a grand effort at examining the gooey slimy mess until one of our owners discovered it.

Then, after much conversation, accompanied by a chorus of ewe and yuck from our humans, would then result in the hairball taken away to a large container. It did not take the three of us very long to learn how to get into the hairball eating container. I once heard one of the humans refer to this as a garbage can. While I knew the word garbage was negative, I felt a rising compulsion to explore why my humans thought the hairballs were better off there.

One day we decided to see why our hairballs were deposited in this container. I was happy enough to provide help for my siblings to learn the trick of knocking over this hairball container, this garbage can. After several rounds of bumping into it, rubbing against it, and putting our paws on it, still no movement. There must be a way so I jumped up on top to get a better look at this hairball eater. I discovered there was a way if I timed it just right. I perched myself on the very top edge and precariously put my front paws on front, next I would jump off while forcing my back paws to push against, which created enough thrust to accomplish the task of dumping out the contents. I was proud to share this newfound knowledge with my sisters and together we could easily explore and find the hidden hairballs. Unfortunately the taste was not nearly as good as when they were freshly hacked.

Once we mastered how to access the garbage can and explore, we quickly learned just how much fun we could have. Especially when the three of us would crawl inside, thus greeted with wonderful smells and some tasty morsels. Unfortunately, though, this adventure also drew unwelcomed attention from the humans, especially as they worked to clean up all the fun we had.

Enough about my siblings, this story is about me. Allow me to fill you in on the most important cat in this story…me…my name is Whitie. My humans were not exactly on the high end of the intelligence score when it came to naming us. Obviously, I am an all-white cat with short hair and green eyes that have the ability to see right into a soul, regardless of whether it is a human soul or an animal soul. My siblings were named Gray and Sparkles. I will allow you to figure out which one is which. It should be relatively easy; especially since it is obvious, a human is reading this. Cats do not read you know. We have much more interesting ways to amuse ourselves. But then again, since this is a human reading this, perhaps I am taking too much into assumption, and should give you a bit more detail about my two siblings.

Gray is an all gray cat, with short fur and green eyes whose stare can deeply rattle most cats, putting them on the defense. She does not have any distinguishing features that would offset her from other felines except her playfulness, which seemed to be almost over abundant. Gray would play as if she could never get enough, fast enough. She seemed to be trying to cram every bit of life into one day, which was every day. The ritual of catnaps were considered nonessential for Gray. Just playing, that was her main event.

On the other hand, there was Sparkles, who had slick, long, black fur, as I mentioned previously, which needed constant attention. Sparkles was always grooming herself and often bragged about being the best-looking cat in the clan. Her eyes would appear as gems, glowing and sparkling even in the middle of the night. There were many times I would awaken in pitch black and be able to pinpoint Sparkles' location from the glow of her eyes. The sparkling eyes were not exactly yellow or green but a rich combination of the two shades, blending together to the point of one appearing as if it were the other color, until they almost appeared to be one in the same. They never appeared dull and lackluster either, but were always staring into you as if she could read your mind. Nerve wracking to say the least. The humans often referred to her eyes as being jewels instead of eyes. Sparkles never seemed to mind and if anything, she would brag to our clan that she had the jewels in the family. I am sure she did not realize that since I was the male cat, that was an inside joke.

As for myself, I did not have sparkling eyes, or nonstop energy. I was no more than an average white, short-haired cat with plain green eyes. I would have been considered by most humans as any old feline. To the contrary, I was the cat with a personality that demanded attention. I was the cat with an attitude, a catitude, not to mention possessing an air of authority. When I walked into a room, other felines moved out of my way, they knew I was the alpha cat, the one in command. I was affectionately named, "The King," but I will get into that later.

<<< TWO >>>

The humans who took care of our every need had unusual names, at least to a cat that is. The man of the house was named Kurt; although, sometimes the woman referred to him as dear, honey, and some other names, she would whisper under her breath at times when she was angry or upset. I had decided that Kurt was mine. All mine. I let him know that I had chosen him early in our relationship. I tolerated the woman, especially when she gave me special treats but Kurt was the one who I would not only live with, but he would be the last one I would see.

The woman of the house, named Beth, had various names too. When the little kids came to visit, they called her Nana. Sometimes the man would call her dear, just like she called him. I never really understood why they wanted to call each other the same name, especially since cats have their own names. However, I suppose that is a right of being a human. Humans make such a grand issue over names while cats are fine with whatever name their humans decide for them. I have determined in my cat wisdom that we will never be able to figure out this whole naming ritual.

Kurt and Beth took care of our every need, giving us food and fresh water, playing with us, and even introducing the litter box. I never really enjoyed the litter box as much as my sisters did, often preferring to sneak out the open door to do my business. The first time I ventured outside it was a brand new world for me. Unfortunately, I did not get to see much of this wide-open space, filled with intoxicating scents and the feel of grass and dirt. Before I had the opportunity to explore, Kurt quickly picked me up by the scruff of my neck and unceremoniously threw me back inside. Fortunately, I was the kind of cat who could quickly place their feet in a landing position. The myth is not true that all cats land on their feet. I was disappointed, yet still determined, that the next time one of the humans forgot to shut that door, it would be my opportunity to resume my exploration. I would make sure the next time; I would be out of Kurt's reach.

The opportunity presented itself soon enough. I had been sitting by the door for the better part of a day and after missing several naps, it happened. The door opened and stayed opened just long enough for me to make my escape into the great unknown.

Little did I realize my addiction for exploring would lead to my ultimate demise, but let me continue.

My first exploration of the outside world was short lived, but this would begin an intense thirst for my life as an adventurer. No, I was not literally thirsty. I can go to my water dish for that need. Unless of course my owners forget to fill it as they sometimes did. When that happens, I can usually convince Kurt to turn on the bathroom sink for me, which I prefer, allowing the cool droplets of running water to quench my thirst. Now I am diverging, so back to the great outdoors.

The first time I successfully managed to sneak outside, I chose to confine myself to the yard directly in front of the house. After all, I was still considered a kitten, and to venture much further from that could possible involve a threat, one I was barely able to contend with yet. The key word here is yet, and soon enough I would be able to fend for myself, which I was always anxious to prove that fact to my sisters. The outside world was one I still was unfamiliar with. Anyways, my humans needed to spoil me, and if I showed them too much independence, well they may not see the necessity to supply my every need. I might be an exploring loving cat but I sure was not stupid. I knew a good thing.

One of my outside activities I soon discovered was the ability to dig holes in the dirt. With this newfound appreciation, I found my every waking moment engulfed with the notion to go outside and dig holes in every conceivable place. Once I had established these freshly dug holes, I quickly realized I could leave my scents in the holes and establish my territory. I was elated with this discovery, while at the same time disappointed to come to grips with the fact that litter boxes were not nearly as much fun as digging in fresh dirt. I loved to dig in the place right outside the front door where fragrant flowers bloomed in excess. Gray and Sparkles did not seem to possess the same desire I had. That is digging outside where all of nature's scents blended into one intoxicating high. Similar to catnip. Unfortunately, Beth did not appear to appreciate my gifts I would leave behind after a day of digging and pooping. Oftentimes, after a day of my outside explorations, I would hear her yell my name, and I can assure you, it did not indicated that we were going to play.

There were also those times when she play in my dirt filled

litter box, resulting in a large basket full of vegetables, the same vegetables that often got in the way of my enormous outside litter box. Beth seemed to get a great thrill from calling me repeatedly, after the vegetable episode, as she ran water in the sink. She kept saying my name and running the water, I was not at all sure exactly what Beth wanted me to do. So naturally, I assumed she needed me to test out the water to make sure it was fresh. Perhaps she needed me to play with the vegetables she was fussing over, although cats were not necessarily a big fan of vegetables. Regretfully, I soon understood that her tone of voice was not conducive to any of those ideas.

"Cats! I hate cats. No, I don't hate you Whitie. I just wish you would stay out of the garden. This is so gross," Beth kept saying in a terse voice.

I could not quite understand why Beth was so angry with me. She kept repeatedly calling me while she scrubbed at the vegetables. I tried eating vegetables once but like I said before the taste was not nearly as delicious as the pieces of meat. Kurt would often give me morsels of meat and cheeses after dinner each night. He always saved me a treat because, well because I was his cat and that is what a human does for his cat. I learned another word in my catabulary, (which is the vocabulary of all felines, unknown to humans of course.) That word was "treats." Cats do learn words from humans, in case you did not realize that. My human kept saying the word treat repeatedly.

"Whitie, want a treat?" He would say as he held out the tantalizing piece of meat in front of my face. That is what I soon learned to call this ritual. Treat. It meant that I would jump up on the kitchen counter (and not being called a bad cat), while Kurt, my human, would reward me for being so intelligent.

Of course, Beth was not giving me any treats at this point in my day, and normally I would love to sit at the sink and drink from the running water. However, during these times, I somehow knew she did not want me there, so when she was involved in the vegetable ritual I decided the best thing I could do was to avoid the place.

We were growing, Gray, Sparkles and I, and as we began to grow the house became even more of an adventure, seemingly multiplying with new locations to explore. I not only encouraged Gray and Sparkles to climb but I told them that every counter, shelf, and piece of furniture were to be mastered. Days seemed to fly by as the three of us mastered these hidden places, and our daily escapades grew less exciting, until we were forced to go outside for new discoveries.

Mastering the territory, alias our home was a rite of kittens growing into cats. However, the humans were anything but appreciative of this feline ritual. They would squirt us with a bottle of water, sometimes even in the face. This was not the same thirst quenching droplets of water that trickled down from the sink, or even the cool refreshing water in our never-ending water dish. Instead the type of water that made our fur an uncomfortable level of wet. Way too wet for a cat's liking. We despised that part about our humans. Why would they get us wet when all we wanted to do was explore? Watered down fur and cats were just not in the equation of feline life.

However, we soon learned that we could avoid the spraying punishment if we simply did not jump on the counter, but when the table held the wonderful aroma of sweet morsels, we just could not resist. When this happened, we managed to only get a bit wet and could easily shake off the water from our fur. One day though, it did not end with us just getting wet. We sat on the floor just waiting for some treat to drop, but when it seemed futile, I finally decided to take matters into my own paws.

I consulted with my two companions before leaping (literally) into action. The smell was just too much for me to silently sit and wait for. Without any regard for the humans, I decided to take a flying leap onto the table, landing right in the middle of a plate full of meat. This must be what the Rainbow Bridge is like, I thought for an instant. I was so excited I began to devour the large plate of meat, ignoring the spray from the water bottle and the screams from my owners.

"Ughh" Kurt yelled. "Get! Get!"

Kurt snatched me up roughly, opened the front door and tossed me outside, soon followed by my two siblings. We sat at the door mewing, but it remained firmly shut. I licked the rest of the succulent meat from my paws and sat looking at my littermates. Technically, they had done nothing wrong and I was the one at fault. Had it not been for me and the overwhelming desire to dive into the meat we would still be inside with our humans. I sat contemplating the entire scene while darkness began to settle.

"Let's scratch at the door. They will have no other option but to let us back in." I told my littermates who were beginning to get a little concerned.

"Whitie, why are we out here? I don't want to explore. It's getting dark," Sparkles looked to me for guidance.

Why shouldn't she? After all, I was the alpha cat, the one in control. At least I should be in control, but now being outside while the door to the house remained firmly shut; even I, was beginning to question exactly how much I could do.

Looking back in retrospect, I ponder the ultimate question that had led us out here, "Why did I have to have that meat?"

Darkness soon covered the ground and we were about to give up going in for the night when the door creaked open and out came Beth. She petted us and spoke softly, positioning herself on the porch floor so that we could circle her and rub our scents onto her skin, showing that we stilled cared. When minutes later she got up, we assumed it was to let us inside. To the contrary, she left us astonished, as she simply slid back into the house taking away all hope of us going back in.

This was a new and frightening series of events which, unfortunately, we were coming to the realization, that this would be the first time we would have to spend the night outside. Soon the knowledge that the great outdoors could be unkind was more than a fleeting thought. It was our newfound reality. We quickly understood, more or less, and especially because of my own greediness, that this was going to be our demise. I joined my siblings as the three of us gazed at the door anxious to go back in, even crying in earnest, but that just simply resulted in the overhead light turned off. Thus leaving us in complete darkness.

Gray decided to use my giant litter box with the fragrant smelling flowers growing in it. She skirted off the front porch, by mounting the steps one at a time. As soon as she hit the bottom she instantly began digging in earnest, of course after sniffing out one of my previous scent markings.

Meanwhile, Sparkles just seemed to be in a state of total confusion pacing back and forth between the door and the spot where I had decided was going to be comfortable, for a night's sleep. She kept mewing softly, what was she thinking? She felt that if she just cried, in a tone imploring help, that the door would magically open?

"It's not so bad out here," I bragged to Sparkles, all the while I was forcing a raging mew back down into my throat.

But, I knew that no matter how much a cat cried, doors just did not open, and that the gesture was just an exaggeration in energy, nevertheless she continued. Ah let her, I thought to myself, I am too tired to care. I closed my eyes as I curled up into a tight ball trying to adjust to the night air, which had begun to turn a bit cooler, just faintly acknowledging that Gray had scampered back up onto the porch and had joined Sparkles in her cries.

The slight breeze brought with it several scents so I raised my nose slightly to try to filter them out one at a time. There was the smell of food somewhere afar off, as well as the smell of…wait…a dog? No, that could not be. I needed to alert my siblings.

"Hey Sparkles, Gray, do you smell a canine?" I was anxious to get a second opinion.

"Not sure Whitie. There is an odd scent though," Gray raised her nose to the air and began to sneeze, a feline's result of trying to smell more than possible.

I tried not to join her in the sneezing episode but I could not help it. Cats simply had to mock each other, a unique quirk we have, and something again humans will never understand. In a way, it is instinct I suppose. The way we acknowledge each other's presence and inform other felines that they are important enough to be accepted. Humans, on the other hand, insist on doing their own thing, and often will do the opposite of other humans. I tried to understand that, but never would.

Now I had to concentrate on that distinct canine odor. Dogs often mean trouble, big trouble for cats. I must be on alert and prepared to defend my territory if such a danger presented itself. I must stay awake; I continued to tell myself even as my eyes began to close. I must…

I had no concept of how long I had been asleep when suddenly I was alerted by something I knew instantly was trouble. Upon opening my eyes, I saw the reason for my sudden state of panic, a large bird of prey, staring at all three of us from the banister of the porch. Gray and Sparkles were already on alert, standing straight with their fur full, tails up, and ready to attack.

10

Needing to show them that I had already knew about the danger, I slowly rose up on my back haunches and of course, being the most curious of the clan, I slithered my body toward the bird. He sat with his eyes wide open, staring. His claws extended. We were still small enough that I knew if he wanted to, he could easily carry any one of us away. Yet, I still was too curious to be frightened, or even wary of that dangerous fact.

His mouth opened and a most unusual sound came out, not a bird chirping, but more of an extended howl. I thought in my adventures that I had heard every bird sound there was. However this was one that not only was strangely new, but one that left me panting with anxiety. I had never heard a bird howl like that before and instinctively knew that this was not the usual bird I had annoyed and chased in the yard.

Looking around I also realized that those birds, were nowhere to be seen I was suddenly more than curious why this large bird of prey was out so late at night when the other smaller birds I had played with during the day were obviously missing from this crazy scene. Mulling back on those birds I suddenly felt a deep sorrow for making their lives so miserable, with my need to hunt and conquer.

Just as I had begun to assimilate this new information, the overhead light suddenly illuminated the entire situation, and apparently the bird was not as appreciative of having light cast onto the environment, he spread his huge wings swooping away. No sooner had the bird of prey taken flight, than the door opened and Kurt appeared. He was looking past us at first and then his eyes turned toward the cats as he seemed to be closely observing the felines forced to sleep on the porch. He held the door open and we three wasted no time in running straight into the house, glad for the comfort of the inside.

Whatever the game, we had been forced into playing on the front porch, was thankfully over now, and we didn't mind sharing the as we drank thirstily from the water dish. With our thirst satisfied one by one we began sprawling out on the floor enjoying the comforting sounds of the house. The hissing of cool air was a strangely comforting sound as the wind blew from an open window.

Although I could still smell the scent of that mysteriously large bird, I no longer worried about what he might do. The ticking of the clock in the room next door was in perfect rhythm to Kurt's long deep breathing. I could hear Beth tossing back and forth and the sounds of her mumbling about not having room, were a comfort to me, as I began to nod off to the familiar sounds of the house at night.

My dreams were soon consumed with the large bird, and in my dreams I was running as he came swooping down upon me. I dreamed I was gathered into his large claws as they were piercing my sides, burning a searing mark into me. I found myself jerking as hard as I could, but not hard enough to free myself from his talons. I had literally jerked myself awake realizing that Gray was kneading me and push her gently away, but I could not erase the dream from my mind. The bird was alive in front of me as I shook my head to try and rid the enemy from my eyes.

I stretched myself wider awake knocking Gray over on her side, where she instantly decided, was the most comfortable position to sleep. She gazed at me through slightly hooded eyes and mumbled, "Good night Whitie."

After a round at the food dish, I had already forgotten about the large bird, and even refused to dwell on the weird outdoor game my humans had insisted I played earlier tonight. Whatever was wrong with them obviously was no longer a problem. I made up my mind that I refused to consider what had happened earlier, and convinced myself that for tonight at least, I would be content to use the small inside litter box to deposit my treasures, and not worry about scratching at the door to be let out, into the gigantic outside dirt filled litter box. I sprawled out on the soft carpet and began nodding off to sleep. I was grateful for the soft carpet instead of the rough wood of the porch. That was my last waking thought as I gently closed my eyes.

Sometime later that night, I was roused awake by an odd feeling, and was drawn to the low hanging window. I crouched in a tiger like motion, making my way over to peer out the window; where I saw him again. The large bird of prey was now sitting high up in an overhanging branch that appeared to be shadowing the entire front yard. I sucked in my breath with an urgent need to suddenly protect my sisters.

It was then I realized that swooping creature had the nerve to be staring down at me. The scrutinizing, intense look he gave, made me shiver despite the obvious fact that I was protected inside. While that satanic like creature could not get in. I took a silent vow then and there that this mysterious bird was one not to be reckoned with; and that for some unknown reason I felt the need to warn my siblings. I went in search of them only to find they had both curled up on the bed with our humans.

I jumped into Kurt's arms, and he rolled over and snuggled me. That was exactly where I needed to be at this very moment. It was at this point in my life that I chose Kurt as my soul mate. He was mine, and cats choose their owner, not the other way around. I slept contently in his arms knowing that for the rest of my life I would be dedicated solely to Kurt. I would vow to be his cat and would make sure my owner was pleased with me. This was my desire in life, and little did I realize that I would impact his life long after I was gone.

<<< THREE >>>

The next morning began as most days with the strong aroma of coffee, a drink humans seemed to relish, while cats, not so much. Of course, there was an exception to that, but only if I could get to Beth's coffee right *after* she poured the sweet cream into her cup, and then I had to pounce on it right *before* she poured the aromatic, rich coffee. I tried gulping down the sweet cream, but learned after only one episode of this was Beth's reaction escorting me off the counter, with a squirt of water and some terse words. Kurt's coffee was not nearly as intoxicating as Beth's though. His was strong and lacked the aroma of sweet cream so I was not at all interested in pursuing his morning coffee.

This morning though both of our owners appeared to be in yet another state of frantic panic. Over the short time we had lived here, this panicked stricken routine seemed to happen most days.

Of course, there were those mornings when the pace was much slower and more to a cat's liking. When these days happened, we would enjoy sleeping late long into the morning with our owners. The pace appearing to be much slower. More to the way cats take on life.

However, humans are more complex than cats and it is a sad state of frazzled complexity that humans force themselves to live. "Why couldn't they just learn from cats?" I pondered. "If everyone woke up like a cat then there wouldn't be any reason to move about so quickly, not to mention way too early to start a cat's day." The panic ended, as it did most days with first one and then the other human dashing out the front door.

Occasionally there would be those treasured moments when our humans would take some extra special time to pet us before leaving. However, more often than not, they would simply leave without so much as a glance our way. While my siblings seemed unaffected by this, I was always at odds with the situation. After all, I was a good cat and deserved my share of attention, which in my opinion, was never enough. I needed my long pets. I enjoyed kneading my owner's pants, even if I did sometimes put an ever so small tear into them.

I suppose cats will never quite understand human's need for wearing clothing. Fur should be good enough for every living creature. However, the most fun I had in the early mornings were when Kurt stayed long enough for me to brush up against him, leaving a trail of extra special scents on my human, which lately, I was reluctantly beginning to understand, were rarely appreciated.

Unfortunately, today was not going to be one of those days filled with extra special attention and loving. The door had slammed shut and suddenly all signs of human life had been obliterated. The only reason I could come up with to explain these strange turn of events was that the door stood guard between my chosen human and me. I sat staring at that door waiting for it to open, dumping my human back into the house again but it remained firmly shut. That nasty monstrous door was keeping him from me. How dare that door do that! What gave that piece of wood the right to stand in the way of my need to be loved and my human's obvious need for a bit of my in-depth cuddling? I was after all, the one who had chosen him to devote all of my waking moments to, right? What right did that large piece of plain brown wood have to keep me from those, whose very lives were dependent upon me to enrich them with a love that only a cat could bestow upon a human?

"Purrrrrrr...you like that Whitie? Here let me rub you some more," Gray came sleeking up and rubbed against me, but even that didn't help as much as you might think.

Eventually I strode past the food dish which contained a new type of food combination, having been placed there in the midst of the early morning ritual of fresh food. I was less than fazed by this rich mixture which smelled like it might taste good. My very soul had been bruised for yet another day, with my owners leaving me.

Cats have very little concept of time and we often mix up time. To me it felt like I would die first before seeing either one of them again. Sparkles, who had been sitting in the corner taking a nap, had now yawned and looked my direction asking me why I was in such a state of panic.

"You wouldn't understand Sparkles," I snapped back at her before brushing past her in a huff.

I roamed into the bedroom, after all this was the place where I permitted the humans to sleep with me in a large soft bed, that I was sure was there just for my comfort. I was obliged to share it, for no better reason than the extra comfort that act of kindness afforded me. I pounced my body up on the one side I preferred to sleep on. The covers were neatly organized, so for spite I decided to bunch them up, and then preceded to lay upon the more comfortable pile of covers now, as opposed to the flat ones previously. Eventually Gray and Sparkles joined me and we settled in for a nap.

I wasn't sure how much time had passed, but judging from the way the sun had moved across the house I surmised it was much later and the nap had helped to pass the time. The ache for my humans to show me some well-deserved attention was even more painfully felt. Stretching out my sleek body, I arose from the pile of blankets that had, without my permission of course, lost some of their fluffiness, and decided what needed to be done was to partake of some nourishment.

Upon my approach to the food dish I noticed that my siblings were already digging into the food and quickly changed my mind about eating. After all, I didn't exactly appreciate sharing my feeding time. Instead, I went back to the big selfish wooden door and decided to sharpen my claws on it. Although there were many posts that I could have used, I decided to take it out on the human hiding door that was still harboring my owners behind it.

I tentatively put one paw on the door testing the wood to make sure it was of a good consistency to sharpen my claws and immediately found the activity to my satisfaction. After a few short test swipes, I began to earnestly rack my claws in rapid strokes, then licked each one clean to make sure they were not only sharp but, shinning as well.

Eventually Gray came over to inspect my handiwork on the door and decided to add her claws to the process as well. Before long the two of us were furtively sharpening our claws and I noticed there was a gathering of wood shavings on the floor.

Sparkles joined us but she was not as interested in sharpening and maintaining her claws. Instead she found the wood shavings as a new toy, one in which she could bat around and spread throughout the living room. Gray and I lost interest in the door and decided instead to finish the project on one of the posts we had used before, but Sparkles continued to play with the shavings throwing them up in the air and chasing them, as if they were a predator that she could leap upon and snag for a prize.

The sun was just beginning to fade from the sky when we all heard the familiar noise at the same time. We were being rescued, our owners had just opened the door and were coming home to save us from this horrid predicament we had been left in forever. I was more than happy to receive my fair share of petting and had just jumped up on the counter to continue the episode when Sparkles entered the scene carrying one of the wood shavings in her mouth and dropped it on the counter as an offering for Beth.

Beth stood starring at it a bit confused and then she called Kurt, who not only looked confused, but a bit on the angry side as well. I couldn't fathom why he would be angry at being given such an award, especially since it took a great deal of effort to sharpen our claws to perfection. Regardless he was angry and began to pace the house, suddenly playing a new game of inspecting every wall and every piece of furniture, until finally he came to the door where we had gathered with him as well.

I brushed up against him to let him know that he was more than welcome to sharpen his claws there too and that we hadn't considered it only belonging to us. Somehow, though neither one of the humans appeared very pleased with our day's accomplishment.

Instead of congratulating us, we suddenly found ourselves pitched outside again, with this time being even hastier than the last time. Was this to be our new accommodations now? Outside on the porch, with the large-winged bird of prey at night? I could not image that was to be our nightly plight now. Or was it?

I noticed that Beth drove away in the car and when she came outside she simply brushed past us muttering words that I could not understand as of yet. I was still building my catabulary (which is the words that humans speak and cats come to associate with). Her words spoken in harsh undertones and she did not even acknowledge that we were there. She backed out onto the road and our world became quiet once again, with only the early evening sounds interrupting the silence. The man who walked his dog came by and we hid before the dog had a chance to pull on his chain in a futile attempt to get to us.

The evening had just begun to turn cooler when Beth pulled up in the driveway and proceeded to get a large flat box out of the back of the car. She had just begun to struggle with it, while I was slinking over to see exactly what she was doing, when Kurt came barreling out of the door. The same door he had slammed shut after dumping us again into the evils of nightfall. The same door Beth had come out of and brushed past us. I must do something about that door, I determined.

"Here I'll get that." Kurt said as he swiftly lifted the box out of the car.

Beth followed him in but just as we were going to follow the both of them into the house, SLAM, and that door stood guard again. I seriously hated that door. I decided I would stand there and stare it down, but eventually I gave in and decided to go and play in the dirt filled litter box, scratching furiously, taking out my frustrations with the monster door on the dirt instead.

Unlike the last time, we were eventually allowed back inside but the mood was not exactly friendly, coming from our humans toward any of the felines. Instead, we were virtually dismissed from the evening activities with no consideration to the petting ritual or even playing the newly found red-dot-of-light game, the one where a red dot would bounce on the floors and walls encouraging us to hunt it down. We would chase the red-dot-of-light while the humans found enormous pleasure in watching us. They would laugh as we were perplexed how the red-dot-of-light suddenly appeared and then disappeared. I had somewhat of an idea that the humans were possibly connected to the red-dot-of-light, but had yet to figure out how it all fit together.

Tonight was altogether different in many ways. First, we were forced to spend time outside. Then when we were able to get past the monster door and come back in, we were dismissed from our cuddling time. Perhaps the strangest of all activities was when it came time to go to bed. My sisters and I were put in a most strange place. I noticed most of the evening the humans were engrossed in putting together a large metal box. Not a litter box but one which we could see into. I didn't understand what this was all about but then again most things humans do don't exactly make a lot of sense to a cat anyways. I was more than hurt that tonight Kurt did not spend any time snuggling with me, and if anything, he almost seemed to ignore me.

When it came time to go to bed, I had resigned myself to the fact that I was not welcomed to sleep with my human but I still had to keep him company. I roamed from place to place on the bed, until finally I curled up at his feet, pushing up against them for the small amount of warmth they gave. Lately I was finding that the bigger I was growing the less tight places I could curl myself into and be comfortable. This was no different. I was becoming so accustomed to curling up in his arm and purring contently, but tonight there was no arm available. Denying my human of my purring was the only way I could come up with to retaliate, but that just resulted in me sleeping fitfully. I got up several times that night to search the house, finding nothing worth playing with except the metal container that stood in the middle of the living room.

The next morning the usual ritual occurred with the aroma of coffee and the rushing back and forth throughout the house, except this time it seemed even earlier. My humans played again with the metal box and this time they put a litter box inside. Now I was more than confused wondering why a litter box was put in there. Cats are known to be so curious that it often gets them into predicaments they wish they had not been in, and this was going to one such example of that very concept. I was curious enough, along with my siblings, to go in and explore this situation.

The metal box was smaller inside than it was outside due to the litter box. There was also a bowl of food and water each one being attached to one of the walls. While my siblings and I explored the inside of the box, I caught out of the corner of my eye Kurt rushing over. I thought he was going to join us in the exploration of this new item, then the strangest thing happened. He quickly closed the front of the metal box. I ran to greet my human but instead I discovered that the front was now preventing me from getting to him. Kurt and Beth spoke to each other while I paced the inside perimeter of this metal contraption, which due to the size of it didn't take me long at all. I quickly found myself walking in a tight circle listening to the humans say the word cats numerous times.

Then as we three felines were attempting to assimilate what was happening the front door suddenly closed and we were alone. Only not exactly alone, alone *and* trapped inside this metal box. It had all happened so quickly, that I did not even register the fact the humans had gone out that human eating door. At first we just sat there looking out, then it occurred first to Gray that this was not where she wanted to be. With this bit of knowledge Gray attempted to take matters into her own paws.

What? Do you really think cats take matters into their own hands? That's a human trait, dummy.

She approached the same side we had entered and began head-butting the barrier, not in a loving way but in a way that said she meant business. Even after much pushing and head-butting, nothing changed. We all remained inside.

I decided to give it a try next and figured that using both of my paws to frantically scratch was sure to work. However, after much furtive scratching there was still no budging of even the slightest bit of an opening. Sparkles had no ambition to try and instead she simply crawled into the litter box and curled up. We hadn't used it yet so the litter was clean and it somehow seemed to comfort her as she began to purr. Nothing really affected Sparkles and she was always the docile one, ready to please our humans.

We realized that we were trapped inside of this prison and were tantalized with being able to look around at all the familiar things in our house, yet unable to reach them. I suddenly began to notice how comfortable the couch seemed, yet at the same time so out of my reach. With these thoughts madly running around in my head, I became definite in my decision that I was not going to remain here all day. I starred at the door, the one I had used to sharpen my claws on not more than a day ago, and I could still see the deep scratches I had left by accomplishing such a feat.

Gray had begun her usual meowing when she got upset and her voice became higher and higher pitched with each passing hour. I became tired of trying to figure out this strange change of events and decided to lay down in the corner of this prison, and curl up as tight as I could but still didn't have enough room to really get comfortable. I looked around again gazing in longing at the soft furniture in the room and remembered the soft pile of blankets I had made the day before. I longed to bunch them up again and bask in the luxury of the softness. Gray's voice was beginning to grow hoarse with her constant crying, until finally she gave up begging, even though she sat there at the same wall that had been opened up for us.

I was beginning to feel the urge to use the litter box and I glared at Sparkles willing her to get out of it so I could dig and leave one of my treasures. She appeared to care less and finally when I could wait no longer I nudged her out, beginning my frantic digging. It was embarrassing to squat in such an open place with my siblings mere inches from me but I had no choice. I attempted to cover my leavings as much as I could, but now we all realized there was even less room for all three of us to get comfortable. Now that I had used the litter box, Sparkles no longer wanted to lie in it so we were forced to shove each other against the sides of the metal box, even under the hanging food and water dish which held did not hold much appeal to us at the moment.

I had no idea how long we had crawled back and forth trading places on top of each other, when finally the front door jarred open and in came Beth. She immediately came to us and opened the wall that had eons ago prevented our freedom. I wasn't sure whether to be angry at her or run and head butt her in happiness so I choose a neutral ground and simply rubbed against her leg. I was instantly rewarded with a long pet. Well, I was glad that mistake was over. I'm sure it was a simple mistake and while I would hold somewhat of a grudge against both of my humans, I was almost sure it wouldn't happen again.

Was I ever wrong! The very next morning the same thing happened. Only this time Sparkles was dumb enough to crawl into the metal box but Gray and I had to be caught and pushed inside, while this time it was Beth who firmly closed the door to our prison. To add further insult to the situation some of our water was spilled in her haste to imprison us and now I was forced to sidestep the wet spot. This was simply intolerable. I wailed before Beth could reach the front door. The same door that still possessed our deep grooves from the clawing session. I had no idea where Kurt was, but apparently today he had left much earlier. He must have snuck out this morning before I had even stirred from the nice warm spot he left for me every day when he vacated the bed.

For a moment I thought Beth had realized her mistake, realizing we couldn't stay in here again, another day. She turned and looked forlornly at us. For a split second I thought she might set us free, instead she simply slipped out the door. I was positive that door was evil because it kept taking our humans away. I even entertained the thought that the monster door was responsible for our prison predicament. I would bite that door the next chance I got!

I felt as if the world was ending. Why were we being caged in here? Didn't our humans love us anymore? Of course Sparkles took her spot again in the freshly cleaned litter box. Feeling sour about the entire situation, I immediately shoved her out of it and preceded to leave a smelly big poop. Unfortunately because of the cramped quarters I only partially managed to relieve myself in the litter box, and was alarmed at the realization that some of my poop was now on the floor. What now?

"ROOORRRREEEEOOOWWWW!" I bellowed in a half meow and half native roar. I was a bit shocked at my native side suddenly coming out. It was this metal prison. With the litter box only inches away it seemed to be mocking my situation. Quickly regretting my decision to test the litter, I felt a bit of a regret, realizing all three of us now had nowhere to lay that wouldn't result in being stained with my own smell. I felt guilty and tried to cover up as much as I could by flicking litter out of the box and onto the floor where it laid. But that just resulted in not only litter covered poo being on the floor, but now there was even less area for the three of us to get comfortable. Gray gave me dirty looks and refused to even talk to me, which made the prison even smaller. Sparkles on the other hand almost appeared to be laughing at me and my own embarrassment. Would it ever end? These were my thought as I forced myself to drift, to take a nap. Sleeping, I finally decided, was the only way to avoid the entire scene.

The second day in our prison ended much shorter than the first with Kurt coming home while the sun was still high in the sky. He carried three smaller boxes similar to the one we were confined in but instead of metal they were plastic lined. There was however some metal that resembled our present confinement, in the form of what appeared to be a metal door. We began to meow frantically begging to be left out. He eventually approached our prison and carefully opened the door reaching for us one at a time. I was the last to go deciding to punish my human of contact with me. After all he had left us here and forced me to use a public litter box, without any privacy whatsoever. I had been so engrossed in giving Kurt the reaction I knew he would least expect, that I had failed to realize what was happening to my litter mates until it was too late.

He had forced Gray and Sparkles into separate, smaller, plastic boxes and now I was being force head first into one. The door was quickly shut and it took me only a matter of seconds to tell him off.

"MMEEWWWWWWW," I screamed at my human for mishandling me in such a manner two times in one day. "How dare you," I continued in catabulary that I knew he could not understand, but unfortunately it did little to change this new situation. Looking through the holes on either side of the plastic walls I saw similar traps and discovered that my litter mates were one on each side of me. Gray on one side and Sparkles on the other. I inhaled deeply to smell their familiar scents.

I was so confused. What was happening? I felt myself being lifted inside the box and then the scent of fresh air told me we were going outside. That had to be it. I was going to be allowed back outside to the huge litter box filled with soft dirt. Instead, I found myself inside another much larger confinement which I would later learn was a car. Kurt's scent flowed from somewhere in front of me, so I breathed in deeply attempting to calm myself but to no avail.

I hated this box even more than the large metal prison and soon discovered of all things, there was NO litter in here. What? Seriously? Not only was I trapped in here but if I wanted to do my business I would have to do it and then lie in it. Oh no, not me, not Whitie! I was too honored to even consider that prospect. I hated this plastic, litter-less box with every fiber of my being, only later would I learn how much more the plastic box hated cats.

<<< FOUR >>>

My siblings and I just could not grasp why we were being forced to stay in the plastic litter-less boxes. That's what I instantly called this, a litter-less box. This new prison, one made of plastic, had no cat smells like the delicious ones we enjoyed making and then covering up with our litter. It also had no water or food. Yet we were expected to remain in here? Had my human gone crazy? I heard of humans who beat their cats, tortured them, even to the point of death, but this did not feel like that. At least some of the outside cats I had met told me such stories, I often shuddered at the thought of one of my felines being treated in such a horrendous manner. I tried to reason it out in my head why Kurt had done this to me, to us, but no answers were forthcoming. After all, I was The King. Why would I, Whitie, The King be put inside of this contraption?

Well, I would not be forced to stay in here. I was going to protest, so I began to yowl a long-exaggerated half meow and half howl. I could hear my siblings from both sides start up too. Both of them were demanding to be heard. Sparkles was half yowling and half whining. She sounded much like a dog in pain, whereas Gray's rebuttal to the entire situation was more of a growling howl. Regardless of the amount of noise we three felines created, our owner appeared unaffected by the riotous chorus of protests.

In spite of all our screaming, we continued tossing about inside the plastic crate and we could feel movement under us. I strained my ears to hear Kurt calmly talking as he said, "It'll be okay little ones." But the words, while they were spoken in a hushed tone, did little to comfort me, the brave one, let alone my sisters. Besides they were not words we could yet understand since I had not included them in my catabulary. There was no hint of any of the words I had committed to memory such as: treat, petting, cuddling, litter box, or any other of those words I had learned by now; and litter box simply reminded me of what I needed to do.

Kurt was very confusing and I tried my hardest to understand. Why was I being punished for nothing? We had not left any messes outside of the litter box and our food dishes had been licked clean, so as not to leave any leftovers that would dry and stick to the plate. We even chased the red-dot-of-light the night before making our humans laugh and delight in our play. But all that had taken place before the plastic litter-less prison had been introduced. I couldn't for the life of me imagine what I had done to deserve this. Eventually, I began to tire from all of the emotions being forced from my body, and I dozed off reluctantly allowing myself to adjust to the vibration of whatever was under the plastic litter-less box.

The next thing I knew we were moving, but not in the same way. The vibration that had lulled me to sleep was now missing underneath and actually, it dawned on me, there really didn't feel like anything at all underneath the plastic box. I could smell more humans, more cat smells, and the dreaded dog smell. I forced myself to look out of the part of the plastic litter-less box that had just a short while ago permitted my entrance discovering, much to my amazement, that I was in a brand new place. There were so many exotic smells my nose was overcome forcing a series of sneezes.

"Is that cat sick?" The receptionist asked.

"No...he just sneezes when there are new smells. I guess he's nervous." Kurt replied.

I tried to smell for my siblings but there was no way I could distinguish all the smells of so many animals with those of Grey and Sparkles. I continued to shove my nose into the grates of the plastic box and every time my nose would encounter a new odor, be it a dog, cat, or even a human scent, I would sneeze. Suddenly Kurt's face appeared in front of me. "Are you okay little buddy?" he asked me.

I had no idea what he wanted from me but I could sense the care and concern in his voice and most of all feel the love he expressed so strongly. I forced myself to settle down deciding that the best thing I could do was to lay down and take one of my many daily naps.

I had just begun to dream about chasing the red mysterious dot of light, when suddenly there appeared an opening out of the plastic litter-less box. I quickly darted out only to be scarfed up by a man I had never seen before. "Well look at the beautiful cat!" he exclaimed.

"Don't let looks deceive you," Kurt replied. "He can find trouble anywhere. His nickname is The King and not because of any royalty but because of his attitude."

I jerked my head around to see Kurt standing there suddenly realizing I was on a silver colored table that made my feet slide out from under me. Dr. Dave, I soon learned his name, began looking at my paws, teeth and the rudest thing ever, my rear end. He even probed me there, which took both my human and Dr. Dave to hold me down for. I had never been so mishandled in my life, which really wasn't a long life up to this point. I looked down to see Gray and Sparkles on the floor doing a thorough inspection of every corner probably looking for food or water. It had been a long time since I had eaten or drank anything, and I had a deep thirst and hunger. Why had our owners forgotten to feed us and give us fresh running water from the bathroom sink?

"They all appear to be in excellent health and friendly too." Dr. Dave exclaimed.

"We take good care of them, but this one loves to explore every chance he gets. I have to be careful when the door is opened. He will slip right out and sometimes he doesn't come back for hours." Kurt said and I realized they were talking about me.

I understood some of what Kurt was saying. I did love the outdoors. There was so much to explore. Lately, I would even venture outside of the familiar smells of home. I usually only crossed the street though and the huge dog who lived there could always convince me to run back home where life was much safer. I wasn't afraid of dogs but I didn't exactly adore them either. Lately it seemed, I just couldn't get enough of the exotic smells the outside held for me. I would shake my tail in repayment of Mother Nature and leave my special scent on every blade of grass, stick, and tree I could find. Strangely when I came inside and did the same thing no one seemed appreciative. Beth and Kurt would complain and proceed to wipe the fragrant love odor away. They even replaced my scents with strong smelling chemicals, which of course made me sneeze. I wasn't sure if I sneezed because of the chemical smell or if I sneezed just to show my humans how disappointed I was with their lack of love for my pheromones.

Regardless I wanted to get off this slippery table, away from Doctor Dave's hands, which were beginning to feel less comfortable, and join my siblings. I would show everyone I had the best scents to leave on every wall if I could just move from the hated silver table. Somehow though, I did not think that instinctive behavior would be appreciated at that moment, coupled with the realization that I was getting a whiff of scents that had been left by previous animals and mixed with mine simply would not achieve the same restless ambition that I had been feeling recently. I wasn't sure of all these behaviors, especially since I had begun to explore, and somehow associated it, with the recent weird behavior of my humans.

I had no sooner begun to contemplate all this, than I found myself again being stuffed into the plastic litter-less box. I barely had time to circle around, because again, I went in head first, and before I could put up a protest, the door was slammed shut. I thought for a brief moment about yowling in protest when instead I found myself in transit, to who knows where this time. The smells I was encountering on this trip were even stranger, and while I could smell other animals, I also smelled more chemicals. I began to panic as I tried to find my owner's scent and discovered it was completely gone. He was just here with me, and now I had no idea who was jostling me from side to side, but I knew this human was not Kurt. I began to shake, not a purring type or a cold rattle but one of pure fright.

Eventually my litter-less prison was put down, but I continued to be forced to withstand these tight uncompromising quarters. I tried to stop my insane shaking, an impossibility which finally emitted a small helpless mewing cry. The sound no sooner escaped my mouth when there was a face right in front of me. A human female with a soothing voice began to talk to me.

"Hi pretty one. Are you scared? There's nothing to be scared of. We'll take good care of you." She said as she opened the plastic prison and reached a comforting hand in, urging me to venture out.

This sweet smelling female cuddled me, and I found myself forming my body into her arm. I was rewarded with long strokes, the type of petting that I loved She knew just how to pet me from the top of my head, down my back, eventually ending at my tail. Don't touch the tail, I thought, and somehow she instinctually knew to stop right at the base of my tail.

She continued to do this until I eventually stopped shaking and crying and rolled over into her arms so she could give me a good belly rub. I had lost all thought even wondering where my siblings were until I turned over, suddenly wondering if anyone was petting either of them. The fleeting thought was quickly dismissed as the realization overtook me, that I was so in love with this female who knew just how to make a cat feel in command of his world. So engrossed I was in this newly discovered human that I had not even realized another human had stepped into the room. I felt a prick beside my shoulder, and I realized with a fear unknown to me that another human had just hurt me. It seemed to almost be an afterthought though, because I became extremely tired. Not the kind of tired like time for a nap, but the type of tired I used to feel as a kitten, when Mother Cat would feed us and we would fall asleep in the soft folds of her fur.

<<< FIVE >>>

I slowly awoke from what, at first I thought, was a nap with my mother and siblings but as I became more awake I realize Mother Cat was nowhere near. I was in a strange place that smelled strongly of chemicals and there was very little to see. As my eyes adjusted, I realized I was at the bottom of an almost clear plastic contraption that went around my neck and had my head sitting at the bottom of it. Looking around I wondered where I was, suddenly remembering the ride in the plastic litter-less box and the soothing female human, who was stroking me and rubbing my belly before I went into a deep sleep, so deep I had lost track of all time.

I had no idea what was happening and even stranger, it felt as if my claws were missing on my front paws. Turning my head and looking around, as limited as I could, there was also no evidence of Gray and Sparkles. I was so very confused which just began to get me even more agitated. I was quickly beginning to turn into a grumpy cat and the pain I was feeling was increasing by the second. Fortunately, as soon as my mind began to register the pain, I heard familiar voices. There was no mistaking those voices, my humans were here. How long had it been since I had been with them? My recent situation had left me so traumatized that I had reverted back to thinking I was a kitten again with Mother Cat.

Not only was Kurt here but I also heard Beth. "When had she arrived?" I wondered. She hadn't been with us on the unique ride in the litter-less plastic prison. Normally I'm not as happy to see her as Kurt, but right now I would have been happy to see anyone, including the man who had put the sharp object into my neck before I fell into a deep slumber. I raised my head groggily and there at the top of this huge plastic cone were the two faces that I cared the most about. I tried to show them how happy I was to see them but somehow the commands I was sending to my limbs had no control over my legs so that I slumped over when I attempted to greet my humans. Regardless of my unresponsive body I was so happy to see their faces and Beth and Kurt were so loving. They petted and cooed over me. I was again their loving cat and whatever had transpired to cause these strange series of events

29

obviously was over. Kurt gently picked me up holding me softly so that I even entertained the idea about going back to sleep. Sleep was what I wanted to do more than anything. More than cuddling with my human. More than instructing my sisters on how to explore the great outdoors. More than … well… so much that sleep was exactly what I did. Drifting off to sleep my last thoughts though were disturbing. Where were my siblings? I still could not smell them. I wanted to find Gray and Sparkles but decided that could come later. In Kurt's arms, I decided, that was what I needed. I tumbled down into the darkness of slumber and back to the dream world of being a kitten again, sucking at Mother Cat's teat and curling up in the soft folds of her warm body. Those were my thoughts as I lowered my body into the sweet abyss of a slumbering kitten's world.

When I awoke it was dark. I was back in the house and was very thirsty and hungry. The odd plastic contraption was gone from my neck and I could see clearly again. I struggled to get up and found myself still not very steady and my front paws were sore. I couldn't understand why, but as I attempted to get up I saw that Sparkles lying beside me and we were in the same room where our owners slept. Suddenly it dawned on me that my paws were sore because I was missing my claws. How could this happen? I let out a screaking yowl as I stumbled getting up.

No sooner did I realize this than Kurt was instantly beside me. He gently picked me up and carried me into the kitchen. He was muttering something under his breath. "I'm so sorry Whitie. I didn't know it would be this bad."

I could not understand his words but knew he was genuinely concerned, yet at the same time I felt an overwhelming guilt exuding from my human. How could humans be so diverse with such complex emotions?

He opened the door to the refrigerator and a bright light illuminated the room, while Kurt proceeded to get a delicious smelling item. My nose picked up a heavenly scent while I sat on the counter content, watching my human as he opened a small container and took something out of it. My human gave me a glorious treat of lunchmeat, the rich succulent taste of fresh turkey with just a touch of salt on it. Often we would have these treats but this time it tasted a bit different. It had a slightly bitter taste to it and I was about to spit it out when instead I found myself gulping it down. The second treat was just as good but this time the bitterness was gone, so I quickly dismissed the strange taste as belonging to the rest of the day's odd events and began to lick my front paws to get the pain to recede.

Before I realized my mistake in doing this simple act of wound care, I suddenly found my head at the bottom of the plastic contraption again. Kurt even had the nerve to tighten it around my neck this time making it virtually impossible to slip out. Worse yet, I painfully discovered that grooming myself, let alone licking my sore front paws, was impossible. I let out a long exaggerated half growl, half moan and was picked up and carried to the water dish. I glared at my human. Exactly how was I to drink water with my head stuck down here at the bottom of who knows what? Kurt looked at me with sad eyes and took the plastic thing off. I didn't wait a second and began slurping up as much water as I could take in. When I had finally had my share I sat down, which I quickly realized was a mistake as the plastic trap was immediately put back on.

"Sorry Whitie, but it's for your own good." Kurt sadly admitted to me.

Kurt carried me back into the bedroom and much to my delightful surprise I was placed in a soft new bed that laid right beside my human on the floor. I resolved myself that I was not going to sleep, but instead found myself sinking down again, closing my eyes, allowing the deep slumber to take over. The last think I thought about was how difficult it was to curl up comfortably with this stupid plastic cone on my neck, nevertheless I somehow managed.

Life for the next several days seemed a bit odd. The three felines of the house were each given a bitter treat twice a day but we didn't care as long as it was followed by another piece of lunchmeat that tasted much better the second time. Our plastic cone-shaped neck traps were taken off when we ate and drank but annoyingly put back on immediately after. We were forced to learn how to maneuver into the litter box with these ridiculous looking contraptions around our heads that we couldn't help but stare at wondering if each of us looked half as ridiculous as the others.

Stranger still was how our litter box had changed. Instead of having a soft dirt-like coating in which we could dig, dump, and then cover our wastes we now were forced to do the nasty task in a litter box filled with shredded paper instead of litter. The papers where changed frequently but I missed being able to dig into the gritty dirt. My scents were a bit different too and Gray and Sparkles seemed to be more tired than playful. I too found myself wanting to sleep deeper and longer.

About the time the plastic cones around our necks came off permanently, our lunch meat treats lessened. I sure missed those treats but it seemed as if other things had changed as well. I no longer had the wild desire to shake my tail and leave my special scent on everything. Speaking of that, my owners also had lost interest in going behind me and spraying away my scent with cleaners.

But the strangest of all was my lack of front claws. Where had they gone? Suddenly when I went to scratch on the door it was impossible. The marks were still there but I could no longer make them deeper or create new ones. The scratching posts were still available in the house but it was pointless. Gray and Sparkles too seemed to be unable to leave scratch marks as well. I was tired of contemplating these change of events but I still found myself wanting to explore the outside world even more now.

With the inability to leave my love scents on everything, my desire to explore outside grew even stronger. I looked for opportunities to go outside any chance I got, and eventually Kurt began to hold the door open for me. He seemed to understand my need for exploration even though I felt deep down in my soul he was not happy with my never-ending desire to discover new territories. I embraced this new-found adventurous spirit, but deep down imagined my human encouraged this only because he felt guilty about the traumatic experience we three had at the vet's. Eventually the metal prison disappeared as well. I did however wonder about the small litter-less box and would eventually begin to associate it with strange series of events, about to begin.

<<< SIX >>>

Gray seemed to become less interested every day in playing and her lack of participating in the red-dot-of-light ritual began to affect our humans. Their concern with Gray was beginning to annoy me and I figured the only way I could become the center of attention again was by encouraging Gray to play. I employed all of the methods felines have to entice Gray to get back to her old self but in the end she just didn't seem to want anything to do with us, humans included. Gray's new attitude began taking a toll on our family, especially Beth, who seemed to dote on her more than myself or Sparkles.

Beth began trying to feed Gray special food, when one day they became alarmed at Gray's weight loss. The food Gray was given smelled delicious and once I even got a small taste before Beth quickly shooed me away. Only after Gray refused to eat all of the moist food, were Sparkles and I permitted to finish it. The leftovers increased in portion size as Gray ate less and took longer naps until one day the entire situation became critical.

The litter-less plastic prison was brought out and remembering the last time I had encounter that whole scene I decided that the best thing to do was run. Even Gray managed to take off upon seeing that plastic contraption, but she was quickly scarfed up by Kurt and eventually she was stuffed into the litter-less box. Sparkles and I sat looking perplexed and frightened. We were convinced we were next. The last time was still fresh in my mind so I warned Sparkles, "Run, hide, bite, scratch…umm wait, we can't scratch anymore," I told Sparkles.

I realized Gray was now forced to endure what the humans wanted since she was now stuck in the cage. What was going to happen this time? We had been good cats, eating not only our food but finishing Gray's leftovers too, which were becoming almost like a second meal by now since Gray was eating so little of it. I noticed for the first time how the lack of feeding was beginning to show on her too. Her fur was badly in need of grooming and she had sagging skin. She took longer and more frequent naps and no longer showed any interest in playing anything. All she seemed to want was held and cuddled.

"Gray, you have to get out of there," I tried to remind her about the last time we were forced into the plastic litter-less box.

"I'm tired," Gray forced out. "I want to sleep."

"But don't you remember the last time we were put in these? We lost our claws, and I lost my ability to put my love smells on everything." I felt compelled to remind her.

"You have to get out!" Sparkles screamed behind me.

She seemed almost frantic and I worried that perhaps I was missing something crucial at the moment that only Sparkles could distinctly feel.

"I want Mother Cat," Gray began to cry.

I was more scared at that moment than I had ever been. We three cats had not even thought about Mother Cat for so long that Gray's lament for her shook me to my bones.

"Don't say that Gray. We are big cats now, not baby kittens. We are able to fend for ourselves now. Mother Cat would be angry if she heard you say that." I was becoming more frightened by the minute.

"Mmmmoooottttthhhhheeeerrrrrr" Gray began mewing drawing too much attention from the humans. All they heard was a plaintive cat cry.

Sparkles and I were attempting to understand all of this, when suddenly we saw Gray leaving in the plastic crate as our humans rushed out the front door. Suddenly it was just the two of us, for the first time ever. It had always been the three of us until now. Sparkles began a crying meow and I soon found myself joining in. We cried for a long time, but it did not seem to make any difference. Our voices soon tired of crying for Gray so instead we went into the bedroom to see if, the now two of us, could find comfort in the familiar. The middle of the bed was the most obvious choice for a nap and I even bunched the cover up into a soft pile but even that did not help much. We were still without Gray.

<<< SEVEN >>>

Gray was the quietest of the three. She rarely meowed and even when she did it was always a gentle sound, one that could lull you to sleep instead of causing alert. Gray, our sister, part of our clan, and now she was missing. Taken away in that litter-less, plastic, prison box. Sparkles and I eventually fell into a sleep, but it was a fitful one.

The sun had long gone down and dinner time had passed but still no owners to feed us or clean our litter box. But even worst was no Gray. We were just about to give up on getting dinner when the door opened. Sparkles and I ran to greet our owners and were sure Gray would be with them. We were confused because instead of Gray, our humans came in with an empty plastic box.

I sniffed the box wondering why Gray's scent was painted all over it but she was not there. Perhaps she had gotten out before we managed to see the empty container and she was hiding. An even worse thought swam into my head: maybe she was attached to that plastic trap where a cat's head sits at the bottom of, and she was ashamed to show us.

Beth and Kurt appeared to be moving slowly tonight and I was anxious to be fed and have my litter cleaned. The methodical manner in which they moved about the house was in stark contrast to the rushed morning routine and it was making me nervous. When the two of them eventually sat down, our food dish remained empty. I silently padded over to Kurt not sure about this change of habit and wondered for a moment if Gray had anything to do with our human's strange attitude this evening. Not sure I tentatively put a paw on Kurt's leg to let him know that I was still here and well deserving of my food. Kurt looked at me but not really at me, rather past me and into another world, but fortunately it was enough get his attention as he got up and opened two cans of delicious smelling food. I instantly surmised this was Gray's food and this time we didn't have to wait for her to eat what she wanted. I sniffed Sparkles' can, which was a cross between sweet roasted chicken and some kind of rice taste, which I knew would be good.

I was greeted with an aroma I decided immediately that I had no intention of sharing. A succulent variety of fish instantly overtook my senses. The delicious fishy smell was more to my liking than what Sparkles was given. I loved fish, so much so, that one time I tried to eat one of the fish in the big tank of water. That particular fish did not taste nearly as good as this can of fish, not to mention my owners were pretty upset and the next day there was a cover over top of the water that held the fish and that was a night we were all put into the metal prison again. We thought that prison had been long gone until that night.

Sparkles and I licked the cans clean not wanting to waste a single drop. While we enjoyed our special meal our water and dry food dishes were replenished. Whatever had happened to make our humans so late in feeding us must have been over now. The daily routine seemed to be back except for one very important detail. Gray. Apparently, Gray was not hungry because she still did not come to eat yet. It would not have done her any good though because we had licked our cans so expertly cleaned, even the smell was fading away. She would have to eat the dry food as it didn't appear either Kurt or Beth were going to put anymore canned food out. While I was woofing down my meal it hadn't occurred to me save any for Gray and now it was too late.

Sparkles nosed into the dry food but apparently decided to wait awhile before diving into that food, so she went off to groom herself. She licked intently making sure to get every bit of food off of her face with the use of her paws, eventually licking those clean as well. I starred at her while she cleaned herself feeling like an intruder on her ritual. It was not until times such as these that I remembered our missing claws and regretted allowing my owners to stuff us into the litter-less plastic prison, which I still associated with my missing claws and lack of lover pheromones now. I would kill that litter-less plastic prison someday.

My strong emotions seemed to snap me alert so I sauntered back into the area where my owners were sitting in comfortable chairs talking softly to each other. They were drinking from bottles that smelled strongly of chemicals and I knew this drink would not be very pleasurable to a feline, but for some unknown reason the humans seemed to be enjoying it.

"I'm sure she'll be fine. I liked the new vet and she seemed to be confident Gray would be okay." Beth had just mentioned Gray's name for the first time since they left with her in what seemed to a cat's timing, eons ago.

"Yeah, I'm sure it'll all work out." Kurt responded.

"Yeah....I just..." Beth continued, "Ah, never mind, I just have a feeling, that's all."

"It'll be alright"

"Sure."

My humans' mood was as if something was wrong. Usually they were much more energetic, except tonight it appeared they weren't in the mood to play with their cats. Not even the red-dot-of-light. Mimicking the humans' mood, I chose to jump up on Kurt's lap and convince him to rub my belly by rolling over and over again in his arms, until he was left with no other choice but to rub my belly until I purred.

I casually noticed Beth getting up and leaving the room, so I assumed she had found something better to do. Naturally I assumed she had decided to allow Kurt and me to spend some one-on-one time together. We sat on the chair with me rubbing against him for a long time and eventually he went into the area where they both slept.

I was a bit surprised to see Sparkles cuddled in the bed with Beth in a similar manner that Gray does. I guessed Gray was still hiding somewhere and would eventually show herself, probably in the morning. If Gray wanted to keep herself from the rest of the family then that was her decision. I settled in with Kurt and before long he was snoring, but Beth remained awake. I could tell by her breathing that she was simply lying there and eventually I heard a faint sound that wasn't quite deep breathing but more of a type of human mewing. The kind I verbalized when I was first taken away from Mother Cat. A mournful type of sound. After a while Beth quieted and her breathing became more like that of a human sleeping and the sorrowful noise ceased altogether.

The next morning began a bit odd. My owners slept a bit longer than usual and we were hungry when they eventually got up and began cleaning the litter box. There was still no Gray to be found but somehow I sensed her presence in an odd way. Not the same type of presence that she usually had, this was a more instinctive type of presence. One only a cat can feel. Humans do not allow themselves to recognize that there are deeper ways a cat can be felt to another cat. Humans are just too busy. I had the notion that she was near, just hiding. Beth and Kurt left later than usual and when they got back the strangest thing happened. Both of them smelled very strongly of Gray, but she was not with them. To a human cats all smell the same, but to a cat we each have our own distinct smell. It begins when we are kittens dependent on Mother Cat for our every need. She is the one who determines our scent in order to fit in with the group. Cats have their own method that humans will never be able to comprehend when it comes to smell. Cat's ability to smell is 40 times more than a humans' ability. Felines often mark each other with similar scents to know that we belong together. To a human they simply think we are rubbing up against each other or playing by head-butting. But to a cat that is behavior that is the most social of all. We are sharing and getting to know each other by leaving scents on each other, that in essence, suggest that we are okay to belong together. However, each cat has their own particular scent that says, "I need my space." Which is when a cat knows to steer clear and allow for privacy.

The fact that our humans carried with them Gray's scent made Sparkles and I very uncomfortable. This was NOT how it happened. Cats decided to leave their scents on each other, not humans leaving cat scents on other cats. That was exactly what was happening now, our humans were holding and rubbing against us and Gray's scents were being left on us. The entire situation was very awkward and we both squirmed until finally we were put down and ran to hide and assimilate it all.

Regardless, the humans' moods seemed more normal, they even played red-dot-of-light-game with us for a long time, and they both laughed and laughed. Even though Gray was not here with us to play I wondered if perhaps she would join us and finally come out of hiding. Regardless, I could still feel her in only a way a cat could and even as I was playing and making my owners happy, I still felt an overwhelming sense that Gray was trying to tell me something. I didn't want to stop what I was doing to listen and that would be one of my biggest regrets.

The next day began like the kind I most liked. While our humans were at a slower pace than the mornings when they rushed out the door, they still made sure our litter was cleaned and our food and water dishes filled. We had not been given a can of Gray's food since that strange night and Gray still was hiding from us although while I slept last night I had the strangest dream. Gray came to me and she appeared to be trying to say something. However, when her mouth opened no sound came out. Her eyes carried with her a dark presence and I found myself waking up suddenly trembling in fear of something bad happening but I did not know what it could be.

I heard the distinct sound of the toy my humans held to their ear and talked into. I never could understand why humans enjoyed that toy so much. I tried chewing on it once, which resulted in me being sprayed with water. Earlier I had seen Beth playing with the toy and she seemed happy enough. This time Beth was playing with it in no time and when she returned to the bed she was excited and happy.

"The vet said Gray is good enough to come home today." Beth announced.

I heard the word Gray and wondered where she was. Why was she still hiding? I could barely smell her anymore and even in my dream, her smell was not there. I trotted off to one of the scratching posts, which we no longer scratched but was still great to rub up against for a nice fur ruffling. There was one particular post Gray loved and her scent was still there. I picked up one of the toys with the heavenly smell of catnip and proceeded to throw it in the air acting as if it was the best mouse ever to chase. Still no sign of Gray. Maybe I had heard wrong and Beth did not say her name.

Suddenly I noticed that Beth and Kurt appeared to be moving at a faster speed than they had been throwing clothes on and pulling the covers over the bed. Worse yet, the plastic litter-less prison appeared and was put on the low table in the living room. I sniffed in disdain at it and slightly smelled Gray and when I ventured to crawl into it, there it was, her blanket. Gray loved this blanket and I suddenly began to connect some pieces together but still lacked enough to fully understand. Gray would never hide without her blanket. She pulled it across the floor and loved to roll around on it. Sparkles and I never made a connection to the blanket and Gray's love for it. Gray was never without it, somehow dragging it along with her. Her scent covered every inch of that blanket and I inhaled great gulps of Gray's unique scent. I had almost forgotten that I had voluntarily crawled into the litter-less prison when the ringing sound interrupted my thoughts. I saw Beth darting through the house as I quickly came to my senses, being drunk with Gray's blanket, and darted out of the plastic prison, when the ringing stopped. What happened next I would never be able to understand as Beth began to wail, not just any old wail but one of such intense and mournful sadness it brought everyone instantly to her. I stood there trying to make sense of what was happening with Sparkles looking as perplexed as I was.

"What's wrong?" Kurt demanded.

"The vet's office just called and said they made a mistake." Beth sobbed. "Gray died last night and they don't even have her body."

"WHAT!"

"They thought she was another cat and cremated her," Beth's voice continued to rise scaring the two of us.

"She said Gray," I told Sparkles. "Maybe Gray is finally going to stop hiding. But why are the humans so hysterical about it?

"They are humans, Whitie." Sparkles replied.

"OH MY GOD!" Kurt's scream jolted us into running and hiding, only too bad we weren't hiding as well as Gray because we could still hear their frantic pleas.

"She's dead, she's dead, ohhhhh…" Beth began to wail again.

Sparkles and I quickly surmised that hiding was not what the humans needed right now, so we sauntered over to them, rubbing against them, trying to calm the atmosphere. It wasn't what our instincts told us to do but we knew our humans needed us more than we needed to hide from such emotional shows. We both put as much energy into the rubbing and head butting we could, but still there would be no calming.

Instead, Beth simply sat on the floor and surprisingly picked us up holding both felines to her chest where she continued to wail for quite some time. Although we were both being held uncomfortably, I used my eyes to communicate to Sparkles that we needed to stay with her. Eventually her sobbing slowed until she was just gulping in short ragged breaths. Sparkles and I used that change in atmosphere to scramble away, eventually deciding to find a place in the living room to lay, making sure we were out of the way. We both watched from a distance as Beth pulled herself off the floor and moved toward the plastic prison. We thought perhaps Beth was upset about the plastic litter-less box, but instead of being mean to that prison like I would be she seemed to be doting on it. We cats sat and watched totally perplexed as Beth reached inside pulling out Gray's blanket. She held it to her nose and inhaled deeply, resulting in another round of crying.

"Why is Gray's blanket so upsetting to Beth?" Sparkles was now upset too.

"Who can tell about humans," I remarked. "I would think Gray's blanket would make her happy. I will bite that blanket for making Beth so sad. No! I will bite that plastic litter-less box. That is what is hurting my human."

Beth seemed to calm down after several more minutes of standing by the mean plastic prison holding Gray's blanket tightly against her chest. Could humans really smell the same scents cats did? I wondered. Beth seemed to be able to take in Gray's scent or why else would she simply be rubbing the blanket against herself like that? I attempted to rub against her leg but she still cried. Kurt tried to comfort her as much as humans do to each other but again she cried. After some time, Beth went back to the plastic litter-less box and the blanket and took it to another room.

After that strange day, we never heard the name Gray again and we never saw her either. I had looked in every crack and corner, under every piece of furniture, I even looked outside in our usual adventure spots, but I still could not figure out how she could hide so well. We never saw her eat anymore or come out to use the litter. Eventually Sparkles and I ate the rest of her delicious food until it ran out forcing us to eat the dry food again.

I pondered about Gray. Where was she hiding? Why was her scent slowly fading from the house? Why did Beth put Gray's favorite blanket on a chair and often bring it up to her face? Was Gray hiding in the blanket? I could not imagine how a cat could hide there for so long but what I did know was that she never did return. Eventually I concluded that the plastic litter-less box had something to do with Gray's disappearance and Beth's sadness. I took a silent vow to avoid that plastic litter-less box. It had taken Gray away and I would not allow it to take me away either.

<<< EIGHT >>>

I thought of Gray more often than not. "Where did she go?" I questioned my humans with long drawn-out meows, but instead of answering they would simply stroke my fur with long pets. I think somehow they understood how much I missed Gray and how confused I was that she was gone. As the days went by I came to understand and eventually accept that Gray was not coming back. I was not sure why she no longer wanted to live with us. Even her scent little by little faded from the house. I still looked for her when I went outside on one of my explorations, but she never did appear. Why, I wondered, did she find it so abhorrent here, that she went away?

In a corner of the large closet, in the bedroom, was her blanket oddly still holding Gray's scent. I would sneak into there, roll myself in her blanket and savor in what was left of her smell. One day I noticed Beth sitting on the floor of the closet her face buried into the blanket. "You can smell her too," I tried to communicate to Beth, but instead she simply pushed me aside and threw the treasured material further back behind the pile of dusty rarely worn shoes.

I felt her close to me most often when I curled up in the hidden blanket. Unfortunately as time went on my own scent began to overpower Gray's until even Beth began to realize it. I wondered if humans could distinguish the difference in cat odors and surmised they must be able to, because Beth stopped sitting on the floor and sniffing her blanket. Then one day when I snuck into the closet, I understood why Beth no longer had a desire to smell Gray's blanket. My scent had taken over completely and there was no indication that Gray had even existed. Her scent was gone and I was dismayed to suddenly realize it had disappeared. Beth's smell was most evident in the soft pieces of clothing, dangling from above me but there was no more left of Gray. It was almost as if she was simply leaving one sniff at a time until now when I would have rubbed my nose off just to find her, I had to resign myself to the fact Gray was now history.

I decided to conduct a further inspection of this small room humans called a closet to see why they were so engrossed in here.

Every morning, the humans would spend time, Beth more so than Kurt, as they went through their hurried routine. While exploring in here I made a few discoveries.

On one side it appeared there were fewer pieces of clothing and it was not nearly as fun. This was where Kurt's scent was the strongest, although I caught a slight whiff of Beth too. There were clothes arranged in a rather odd sense of order and even the shoes on the floor were nicely arranged. The other side was a fun sense of complete chaos and Beth's scent covered this side. There were clothes above me, beside me, and yes on the floor for me to bunch up and make myself quite comfortable on. There were shoes in piles and shoes under clothes and shoes hanging in plastic racks that were so much fun to climb on, until one day I knocked one over and was almost buried alive under an avalanche of rubber and leather. This side of the closet appeared to have as much order as a pack of cats high on catnip. I wondered if perhaps the shoes and clothes with Beth's smell coating them had actually gotten into my catnip and had gotten too much. That would explain the chaotic mass on this side of the closet.

Beth seemed to spend a lot of time in the mornings digging through this mess, but somehow she managed to find several different outfits every day and put each one of them on. Then oddly enough Beth would usually throw all but one back, where they often would fall on the floor or even more fun dangle from one of the wooden rods. I would take advantage and hang from one of those pieces until it would slide off and land on the floor with me still hanging on.

Of course I never missed a chance to sniff at Gray's blanket that remained in the closet but her scent was gone so I simply went back to exploring more fun things to do in there until either Beth or Kurt would catch me and throw me out, shutting the door and taking away all my fun. One day I had barely begun my play and was just visiting Gray's blanket when I was thrown out too early.

"Where are you my litter mate?" I cried aloud with a series of meows but no response met my ears. For some odd reason I felt as if Gray was near me and I couldn't see her. It wasn't often I felt this but when I did it was so strong I felt physical pain from missing her. Today I had a strong desire to curl up in her blanket and was angry I had been denied that small comfort.

The next day I wasted no time at all sneaking into the closet when I had a chance, determined to comfort myself this time in Gray's blanket. My initial thought was to find the blanket and take a nap, but my exploration side convinced me instead to see if perhaps there was something better to do first. I decided to see once and for all if these clothes really did like catnip. By now I had grown quite large, with strong muscles that enabled me to leap from place to place. I found that I could actually leap onto a high shelf through the ability of leaping onto the hanging clothes first. I kept jumping back and forth, searching for the catnip and eventually I had knocked so many clothes on the floor that I hadn't realized how much noise I was making until the door suddenly jerked open. Beth was standing there looking a bit confused until she saw me towering above her.

"Get out of there right now!" Beth demanded.

Wow was she looking angry so I decided what needed to be done was to leap further back on the shelf.

"Oh no you don't" she continued swinging her arm back and forth on the top shelf, but she couldn't quite reach me. So I took advantage of her arm and my newly found muscle mass and leaped onto her shoulders which gained me a shriek.

"OWWWW! You bad cat!"

"I'm not bad. I'm The King." I tried to convey by rubbing on her neck as she swatted me to get off.

No longer fun, I decided it was time to get out and go find another adventure. After all, I can't find Gray in the closet anymore. So with that thought I sauntered on out of the room leaving Beth behind picking up the clothes I had knocked down.

I decided to saunter on over to see what Sparkles was doing only to realize she was engaged in a thorough cleaning of herself so I figured it might be better to just go outside instead. I scratched at the front door, gazing at the marks that were still there from when we had our claws. I still was at a loss to figure out where my front claws had gone but was associating it with the strange plastic collar that my head sat at the bottom of. I was glad my humans had gotten over that silly game. Hopefully they would never want to play that game again.

Kurt saw me sitting by the door and he came over opening it to allow me access to the great dirt filled litter box, the one humans refer to as the garden. I was grateful to be able to venture outside for another exploration and rewarded my human with a purr and several rubs around his leg, showing my affection, before I skirted outside. A large inhale of scents told me this time there was something different, instantly putting me on the defense.

I held my head high as I walked out making sure to mark the corner of the bottom step with my scent suddenly stopping dead in my tracks. A strange cat close to my size sat there staring at me. I had never seen this feline before and immediately determined that was the strange scent, so I raised my back end up high, tail standing straight, and whiskers pointed at odd angles forward. I must let this mystery cat know I was in charge.

He seemed unaffected and I began to look this one over. This cat, I had never seen before, had a bushy tail with brown and white strips that seemed to ricochet around his body. We both starred each other down, neither one of us backing down and wanting to break the trance. Eventually this strange cat must have realized he had encountered the alpha male and just slightly turned his head away, acting as if he had seen something more interesting, but I knew he realized that I was The King. Somehow without either one of us speaking, I distinctly understood he was looking for a home. Here! In my territory!

I decided what was most needed was my feigned indifference so I strolled away while at the same time keeping my eye on the stranger to make sure he wasn't invading my territory. After a few more brief couple of stare downs at this interesting cat, I chose to go on an exploration of a new territory. The house next door was always interesting to me with their unique smells and there was a man there who always spoke in gruff tones but somehow I knew he wasn't to be feared. I needed to understand this human too. So I spent a bit more time than usual approaching him this time. I crept up to a metal building that had a pungent odor of something burning.

My eyes were beginning to water, which sent me into a fitful of sneezes, when I came upon the burning stick just lying there, a red light glowing. This must be another one of the red-dot-of-light games, of that I was positive. I was so happy with my discovery. So this is where that red dot kept itself. How amazing, but not unlikely that I, Whitie, had made the discovery. Well, my owners sure would be proud of me for finding it I decided just as I put my paw on it. Immediately I regretted that action as a searing pain raced through my paw.

Screaming, I bounced back. "YYYYYOOOOOOWWWLLLLL I let out a meow that was so unlike any sound that ever escaped my mouth before that it drew the attention of the man around the corner of the metal building. He limped over to me hanging onto a large stick and I wondered if his paw was hurt too from the red lighted dot stick.

I jumped straight up angry at the red dot. It had never done that before. I didn't know at that moment if I was more angry or hurt at that red dot. The pain was almost too much to handle, I had to get away with a searing going through to my leg. The man had a gruff sounding voice as he gently picked me up. I tried to scratch at him to get away but with no claws it was impossible to inflict any danger. His fingers had the same pungent odor as the burning stick. He reached out a tentative hand and asked me a question I didn't understand.

"What's wrong little one?" I managed to slip out of his reach but wasn't so sure he was a danger. My paw was still throbbing but the initial biting pain was easing off now. I backed away from the man not liking the smell of him at all, but found that I couldn't put all of my weight on the paw I had hurt. The pain continued to make simply moving almost unbearable so I decided what might be needed was a good licking. I sat down, not taking my eyes off the strange man while I began tentatively licking my sore paw. The cool saliva felt comforting but the pain still persisted. The man approached me again and I decided to abandon the effort and forced myself to go home

After the red-dot-of-light incident I was too traumatized to remember the strange cat of earlier but as I approached the front door a different cat odor assaulted me. Not mine or Sparkles. Could it be Gray? Did she decide to come back and change her scent? While this smell was slightly familiar, it was still at the same time strange. Deciding what was really needed was to let my sore paw rest, I used the other one to scratch at the door hoping someone inside would hear me. I really needed to lick the soreness away and having to balance myself as gingerly as possible on it was not helping much in the way of pain relief.

The door remained firmly shut so I sat down and began the furious licking again hoping to find some comfort at least in doing this frantic wound healing. I could hear my humans inside but apparently they had no desire to allow me inside with them. Perhaps I needed to get vocal I thought.

"Mrroowww," I tried but somehow my voice sounded a bit faint so I picked up the volume just slightly.

"Mmmmmmrrrrrrrooooooooowwwwwwwwwwww." I tried again, still no response. My paw was hurting again so I gave up and held my paw up feigning some attention to it. Surely my human would see this exaggerated stance.

I'm not sure exactly how much time had passed when the door finally opened. Kurt was standing there looking strangely at me while I limped inside. "Hey Whitie is limping." He announced upon my arrival.

"It's about time," I told Kurt off with a series of meows.

"Well I don't know," came Beth's voice from somewhere inside. "Check him out."

I skipped just out of Kurt's reach intending to make him pay for not answering my call from outside and making me wait. "As soon as I catch him I will."

"Well he can't be limping too much if you can't catch him."

Intent on finding out the new feline scent I half ran and half limped, using the furniture as an quick escape from Kurt's reach. Unfortunately this only caused my paw to begin throbbing again, but I ignored the pain that was coming in short waves knowing what was needed. I had to discover the new feline scent regardless of how badly I hurt. I had to know who belonged to that smell.

No sooner had I rounded the corner and was into the kitchen, the source of all delicious food, when I ran smack into the source. The stranger from outside was here, inside *my* house.

"Whitie, you found your new friend." Beth proclaimed.

Sitting as proud as could be was the stranger cat, the one I found earlier. Now what was he doing here? After all this was my house and I was The King. I was the one who decided who lived here. I hadn't granted permission for this stray cat to come into my home. Yes, he was a stray I immediately established.

"Beth, what are we going to do with this cat?" Kurt said joining me in the kitchen.

"I don't know, we can't just leave him outside, he already used the litter box so he must be someone's cat."

Whatever the conversation was about, I was not happy with any of this so I decided to find out for myself.

"Hey stranger," I spoke in short meows punctuated with partial growls and partial mews. "This is my place. What are you doing here?" I began questioning this stray.

"I'm hungry. Where's the food?" This newbie dared to question me.

"The food is mine." I challenged by backing up and growling, the pain still plainly visible in my stance. I held my tail up rigid letting him know in no uncertain terms he would have to ask me to eat.

"Hey, don't be so mean. I'm just hungry." The stranger showed his submission by putting his ears back and lying his overabundance of fur flat, making his stripes appear to intertwine into a blur of brown, black and white.

Sparkles, not wanting to be left behind in this conversation, joined me by rubbing up and down my entire length, but I was in no mood for her either. My paw was still hurting and now there was this new feline in the house. If my nose was right a male too. I was the male cat in the house, how dare he assume he had the right to be here. As I was registering the sudden changes, Kurt took advantage of my inattentiveness to him and quickly picked me up setting me on the counter, and before I could stop this, he grabbed my sore paw causing me to recoil in pain.

"It looks like he burned it." Kurt declared. I tried to break free but he had me by the scruff of my neck so there was little I could do but hiss and show my teeth. "Easy Whitie. No one is going to hurt you."

"Huh?" Beth was getting the human's food ready and the aroma suddenly reminded me that it was time for me to eat too, as I suddenly realized how hungry I had become with the adventure, and being hurt by the red-dot-of-light. Kurt was not letting go of me.

"It's burned. Silly cat. How did you manage this?" Kurt continued to examine my sore paw causing even more pain. I attempted to nip at him to make him stop but he was too quick for me and loosened his grip on me just enough for me to escape.

Jumping down I made my way over to the food bowl only to make a horrible discovery. My food dish, being occupied by Sparkles was bad enough, but this new cat was also eating from it. I hissed violently and shoved my body into the newbie forcing him to move aside. I was going to make sure he knew that I was not going to share my food with the likes of him. My alpha male cat catitude did absolutely nothing as he continued to eat. I watched in dismay but at the same time realizing he was eating like he hadn't been fed for days.

Regardless of this thought I swayed back and forth keeping him out of the food until I was certain I had my fill and then stepped aside to allow him what was left. I found myself pitying this stranger and eventually rubbed up against him letting him know as cats do when they are accepted.

"Go ahead and eat," I told him, this time with a hint of acceptance. "After all you really don't know when you will eat again."

"Yes, my friend, it's been a long time since I was satisfied." He spoke in hushed tones still leery of being able to have permission to eat in my house.

Realizing how selfish I had been for really no good reason, I decided to go find a good spot to nurse my still sore paw, and crawled under the table for some privacy. The pain wasn't as bad as it had been but it was still quite uncomfortable. After some furtive licks I decided instead to leap up on the bed where I would be more comfortable.

I felt compelled to do the territorial circling of my spot. Humans assume only dogs do that but cats have instincts that are even stronger than dogs. It's a throwback from our ancestor's days as wild cats when they had to worry about something as simple as a place to sleep. I was told these stories of old from Mother Cat, who was told by her Mother Cat, and so on. The dangers our ancestors faced could be as simple as lying down to nap, without first checking for hidden dangers lying in wait for a feline. A poisonous spider could mean a painful death for a cat of ancient times. Grateful I did not have to encounter those dangers, I still was forced to carry out the ancient rituals. That was my last thought as I flopped myself down, licking my sore paw before I fell into a deep sleep, probably exhausted from such a stressful day.

<<< **NINE** >>>

When I awoke, the room was in darkness so I knew the sun had gone down and I had slept for a long time. I wasn't sure how far into the night it was but apparently I hadn't slept too long because I could still hear the sounds of my humans moving about in the house. I heard running water and went to investigate. My paw was feeling much better but I was still wary of putting all my weight on it. I walked with a slight limp but not nearly as bad as before the nap. A nap always helped everything. I can't imagine why humans don't nap more often. They always seem so busy doing stuff that cats find no reason for.

I walked into the bathroom where I heard the sound of running water and jumped on the edge of the bathtub. I noticed with disgust that Kurt was sitting in the middle of the water and of all things there were bubbles forming all around him. I often enjoyed strolling around the bathtub while he was in there but the thought of getting wet, made me cautious, especially with my paw still hurting. For checking on my human he rewarded me with a long pet. His hand was wet but I did not mind much. I considered it similar to a human cleaning me. My master could pet me in just the right spot causing a purring frenzy. The bubbles were just beginning to cover his toes, when from out of nowhere a streak of fur came flying past me landing right in the middle of the bubbles. I freaked out and darted out of there as quickly as possible to avoid the splash of water that just managed to land in the center of my back. The last sight and sound I had was of the new cat and my owner's howl.

"UGHHHHHHH!" I heard bellowing from the tub.

Beth came zipping around the corner and stopped in amazement, unable to believe what she was seeing. There sat Kurt in the bathtub holding onto a cat that was obviously infatuated with the bubble bath.

"What are you doing with a cat in the tub?" Beth demanded holding back her laughter, but not doing a very good job of it.

"I didn't, he jumped in. Get him! NOW!" Kurt demanded back.

A hysterical sound of laughter escaped from Beth that she simply couldn't stop. Kurt sat in the tub glaring at her while hanging onto the cat and the water continued to flow making more bubbles. The crazed cat tried to claw his way back into the tub with an uncontrolled need to play in the bubbles. His paws were frantically clawing at the increasing bubbles, just barely able to attack and pop a few.

"Do you think you could get this out of here before I get clawed?" Kurt was sounding even more annoyed.

Beth, still laughing, grabbed the dripping wet cat dropping him onto the floor. The feline looked back seemingly undecided on which way to go, suddenly making up his mind and running out of the bathroom, spraying a trail of water and bubbles along the way.

After that strange night, the stranger decided he was apparently going to stay. The first couple of weeks he never went toward the door even when it was opened for me to go out on an adventure. I would patiently wait for him but he simply stared at me, almost daring me to go and allow him in charge. Well that was not about to happen I let him know one day.

"Listen stranger." I began.

"Sweetie. The humans have named me Sweetie," the strange one replied.

"Sweetie? Oh yes, the weird naming ritual. I will never understand that part about humans." I told the stranger, Sweetie. "You need to understand one important part of this arrangement." I continued to educate this odd one. "I am in charge here. Got it?"

"Of course, Whitie. I'm just happy to eat and take naps. I've explored. You enjoy. I will just try out some of this awesome catnip here." Sweetie ventured toward my favorite mouse toy.

"Hey that's mine."

I grabbed the toy away making sure to show him just how fun it was. No sooner had I selfishly done that, than I saw the resigned look on Sweetie's face as he sat there watching me have fun. I felt so bad that I decided what needed to be done was allow him to enjoy my toy. I pushed the toy over to him and when he refused to bat at it I reinforced my point by grabbing it by the tail and throwing it, bouncing it off his head. Sweetie continued to gaze at the toy until I understood what he was waiting for. My acceptance.

"Sweetie, if you want to hang out here you have my permission." There I had finally done it.

With a low bow Sweetie accepted. "Thank you my friend. I will make myself worthy of joining the clan." He grabbed the mouse toy and began to throw it up in the air totally engrossed with the act of playing.

It was a few days later that I began to question my owners choice of names for him. Sweetie? What a name for a cat. But at least this time the name did not relate to any part of his shade of fur or the way his eyes sparkled. Perhaps my humans were finally getting wiser in their choice of names, but I couldn't imagine how sweet a feline could be when all he seemed to want to do was chase me and lap up the food preventing Sparkles and I from getting first dibs on the tasty morsels. I had begun to question my decision of accepting him into the clan. I suppose he was here to stay so I might as well help him adjust to the life. The first thing he needed to do was learn to explore the wonderful outside litter box.

The first chance I got to show him the great outdoors proved another challenge of the pecking order. Sweetie seemed to want to do his own thing, which included immediately leaving the yard and venturing way beyond the furthest area I had ever explored.

He ran several houses away and I had to make the decision to turn back when we were almost out of sight of the house. I wasn't in the mood to follow him and perhaps he had some other family who adored him more. One could hope. I had just finished covering up my treasure in the outside dirt filled litter box when Sweetie silently appeared behind me. I jumped straight up and when my feet hit the ground I initiated the chase, letting him know that type of behavior was not going to be tolerated. I nipped at him and we rolled over and over in the grass, snarling and clawing each other.

"*RAOW!*" I was determined to establish my place in this clan. *RAOW! RAOW! RAOW! RAOW!*" I put my front paws into his chest holding him down. Towering over Sweetie. Unfortunately there was just one problem. My front claws didn't work as well as his so after few useless attempts at clawing Sweetie, I abandoned the aggressive fight to saunter off toward the door. Looking back I recoiled in horror. After my aggressiveness I was forced to realize the cold truth. Sweetie was following me. The door opened. (My humans must have known I was ready to go in.) Then the horrors of horrors happened. Beth ignored me and went to Sweetie petting him and cooing.

"Why here you are, I thought you had left us," she spoke with such compassion in her voice it made me want to go take a nap.

I looked around for Kurt thinking perhaps he was happy to see me but he was nowhere in sight. As I entered the bedroom, I gazed at the soft comfy bed which was calling me for a nap, but at the other end of the room there was the sound of running water. Perhaps the sink was running for me to get a fresh drink. I loved when Kurt would turn on the sink and let me lap at the running water. There simply wasn't anything better than fresh running water, except perhaps a nap in the soft folds of the bed in Kurt's arm. Darkness began to overtake the bedroom luring me to jump onto the bed in search of Kurt. I was tired from my adventure, but even more so from having to show the newcomer who was in charge. I jumped up looking around the bed for Kurt, sure he was there. I was ready for a nap and it was his job to be waiting for me, arms available to curl up in. Oddly though when I jumped up and looked around he was nowhere to be seen.

This was not going to work so I ventured toward the sound of the water. I approached the room and out of the nowhere I was knocked over by a crazed cat, Sweetie. I heard a splash and a scream. Well not exactly a scream more of a roar of a human. The type of sound that always make cats run. I ran from the room knocking headfirst into Beth's legs and she let out a wail too. Were all the living creatures losing their minds? I wasn't planning on staying around for any of this. I ran for the front door determined that was the safest place, but as I screeched to a sudden halt at the door realizing there was no escape. I dove under the couch instead, ramming headfirst into Sparkles who was also shaking from all racket.

"Whitie, help!" Sparkles nipped at me out of pure fright. "Have our humans gone mad?"

"I don't know Sparkles. I think it's the new cat Sweetie. He has brought bad luck to us." I was at a loss now and that was not the way The King acted. We heard noise coming from the bathroom and quickly decided that instead of hiding what needed to happen was an evaluation and that wasn't going to happen under the couch. I nudged Sparkles and she knew too what had to be done.

"Get it out!" Kurt was yelling.

"Why did you put him in there again?" Beth was more than

irritated now.

"I didn't. He jumped in."

"Ok, right, sure, whatever you say." Beth just didn't believe him. "No cat likes water."

"Will you just get him?" Kurt was now so irritated I could feel the emotions coming off of him in waves I didn't care to be near.

Beth took Sweetie who had dove head first into the tub and proceeded to shut the bathroom door. Sweetie sat there looking at me as if I didn't understand that every cat enjoys a good bubble bath. That was when I made the final decision, that Sweetie was one to steer clear of. Apparently he was not 100 percent of the feline ancestry as well as lacking a few basics instinct that no one would be able to teach him.

Not long after that screaming incident in the tub, Sweetie did it again. Only this time Kurt wasn't in the bathtub. Sparkles and I starred uncomprehending as both of our owners stood there gazing at a cat. Sweetie was in the bathtub, water running, playing in the bubbles. The bathtub slowly filling with Sweetie backing up, but eventually he allowed his paws to experience the water gingerly trotting toward the faucet and amazingly put his head under the running water.

Sparkles and I joined our humans by sitting on the edge of the bathtub humiliated to admit Sweetie was a part of animals known as cats. Not a single living soul in the bathroom could fathom why a cat would allow themselves to do such a thing. Regardless of whether or not we understood any of this, there was Sweetie, in a bathtub slowly filling with water and bubbles as two amazed humans and two embarrassed cats all sat watching. I would later regret never really getting to know Sweetie better.

Soon my world would be filled with even more cats and little did I realize that the next ones to be introduced would be so dependent that without my help they wouldn't stand a chance. I suppose that is what The King does best in a crazy household. He assures that all is well in the clan, and my work was just about to really begin. Soon I would begin wondering exactly how many of these cats I would have to help my humans rescue. Perhaps it wasn't the cats who needed rescuing as much as the humans needed rescuing from the cats. When would these humans of mine ever stop taking in cats?

<<< TEN >>>

I eventually came to accept that the cat population would increase. One of those times occurred quite suddenly and without any warning. Beth came home in the middle of the day, interrupting a good nap I was taking. Her being home so early was unusual, especially since the cat population had adapted to not seeing either one of our humans before the sun's warmth was beginning to fade, and shadows would form across the living room windows.

Wrapped up in a blanket were two kittens. They were so little that mewing was an effort of pure determination for them. Beth seemed so overly concerned about them to the point that she virtually ignored us when we attempted to investigate what all the fuss was in the blanket. The kittens were so fragile that I decided immediately the best thing I could do was to give them a wide berth. Surely their Mother Cat was around since they were obviously too young to be without her. With that thought came the sudden realization that there had to be another cat nearby. These kittens needed their Mother Cat. Where was she? I needed to find that mother and let her know who was in charge.

Unfortunately, that started me thinking again about when I was a kitten. I had almost forgotten about being one and how I was dependent on Mother Cat for my every need, it was so long ago. Mother Cat, I wondered, where was she now? Did she miss us? Was Gray with her? Perhaps that is where Gray went.

I remembered the day we were taken to the shelter. Put into a cage and forced to watch as people passed us by. Mother Cat did not seem concerned at all and simply laid down in a soft blanket toward the back, away from the strangers who took care of us. But not me. I was going to get as close to the action as possible. I kept putting my paw out, batting at anyone I could, until one day he came.

Kurt. Not only did he stop and pet me but before I knew it he was lifting me out ever so gently and looking me over as if examining me for some unknown trait I might possess. From that day forward, I was a part of him and he was my human. The fact that Gray and Sparkles followed along were merely coincidental.

That was the day we three siblings were taken out of the cage. That also happened to be the day that Mother Cat was left all alone. I never saw her after that. But for some reason, I could not quite understand, I felt Mother Cat's presence was no longer here on earth. As strange as it may sound to humans, cats have the ability to comprehend what humans never seem to bother to take the time to acknowledge. The day we went home with Kurt, I knew Mother Cat's days were not long on this earth. She was soon going to cross the Rainbow Bridge. Perhaps it was the hushed tones of the woman who fed us. The tones that comfort a cat who is getting ready to cross over. I just knew, that I knew.

Suddenly I understood where Gray went. She was no longer here on earth and the sudden realization sent a shiver of terror through me. I remembered the last time I saw her. She was being stuffed into the plastic litter less box. The box took her away. I would hunt down that box and I would destroy it. That box took my sister away from me. I would never be put into the box again. I was the chosen one. These kittens had brought back a memory I thought I had long ago buried.

I looked back at Sparkles who had decided she needed to investigate further into the kitten box. Beth was busy opening a can of milk that smelled strangely similar to the same milk that had leaked from Mother Cat and provided nourishment for all of us. I quickly banished that from my mind. I could not continue down that path. The memories needed to be categorized. Put to rest. I needed to direct all of my focus onto these kittens who needed to be comforted.

It only took a second for my attention to be interrupted with the sounds of Beth cooing at the wee ones. They were struggling with something in their mouths. I realized it was a nipple that held the milk and Beth was holding the miniature milk filled containers. One of the kittens were eating and there was no Mother Cat to feed them. I stood there amazed and wondered how this could be. A kitten needed a mother cat to feed them not a human and yet this kitten was ravenously eating from this odd shaped container.

I sat focused on this mystery and had not even heard Kurt until he had shut the door announcing he was home.

"Hey, Beth. What are you doing home so early?" His voice trailed off as he stopped dead in his tracks upon seeing the kittens held by Beth. "What is that?"

"Their mother died and one of the officers called me at work asking if I would take them. Said he heard we take in strays," Beth responded nonchalantly while continuing to feed the smallest one, a solid black cat with paws that were larger than his head.

"We don't take in strays," Kurt responded.

"Well what was I going to do let them die? They said they were going to take them to animal control where they would be put down. I just had to bring them home," Beth was sounding desperate now.

"They're too young. They'll never survive."

"Well I'll get up tonight and feed them. See they're taking the bottle I got."

"Here, let me see one." Kurt grabbed the other as his hand overwhelmed the kitten.

Most of the night was spent with Kurt and Beth ignoring us and concentrating on the kittens. They seemed to want to eat without really getting full. I guess kittens were like that and they seemed to take up all the time that my humans were supposed to be spending with me. First Beth and then Kurt would get up taking turns preparing the special bottles and feeding the kittens. It was annoying to say the least. I decided the best way to handle the entire situation was to give my humans the brush off.

Unfortunately my idea did not last for long and I found myself needing to check out the newcomers. One of the kittens was an array of different colors that seemed to mix together so much so, that it was difficult to see where one color started and the other began. The other one was solid black with dark eyes that appeared to tell a story that only he knew and wasn't willing to share.

"I'm telling you so you better listen," I began. "I am the one in charge. I decide if you stay. Got it?"

"Meewwwweee" was the only response. Still too young to communicate clearly. Geeze, I thought to myself, not only was I going to have to put up with these annoying kittens but I was also going to have to play Mother Cat and teach them everything a decent cat needed to know. Meewwwwwweeee? I don't think so.

The days and long nights continued, Kurt and Beth became less and less involved with the kittens and life slowly returned to normal. Eventually the kittens began to drink less from the bottles and more from small flat dishes that held the milk. Sparkles, Sweetie and I all attempted to drink the milk but each time we were shooed away.

The names Trouble and Bear began to take over the words baby and kitten. I realized that the kittens were being given a name just like each of us had. Trouble was the tortoise shelled cat whose colors ran into each other. Trouble certainly fit her name since her personality was to seek out trouble of some kind. If she was not knocking down something or running over one of us, she would deliberately made something turn into a problem.

Bear was less active but still enjoyed drinking from a bottle when he got the chance. His front paws would grab that bottle and they seemed to be much larger than his size. Beth kept commenting that he had bear paws, and for a while I thought his name would be Bear Paws but soon a shortened version of simply Bear became his name.

Bear and Trouble grew despite Kurt's initial assumption that they wouldn't survive the first night and before long they began feeding at the food dish and using the litter box. I guess I would have to show them the great outdoors when they were big enough but for now the three of us, Sparkles, Sweetie, and I were content to be the great explorers.

<<< ELEVEN >>>

Trouble and Bear were as different as night and day. While Trouble preferred to stay indoors and the mere thought of even venturing outside with the rest of us was loathsome to her, Bear on the other hand darted outside so much that our owners soon gave up trying to keep him in the house. His paws were so oversized that he looked like a freak, a misfit in the cat world. His paws just seemed to keep growing at twice the speed of his body and we often made fun of him.

"Look at the paws on him."

"Hey Bear, I saw your paws coming before I saw you."

But he didn't seem to mind one bit, and if anything he often used those monster paws against us by swatting us around. The kitten that wasn't supposed to live was sure making up for the doubting humans.

Trouble on the other hand was small, and seemed to be a bit on the weaker side. She was beautiful with her tortoise shelled fur that seemed to never be the same color each time you looked. Her fur was a mass of multiple colors and they seemed to blur into each other making it difficult to really tell her true shade from one moment to another. If you looked at her from one angle the array of fur would appear whiter, from another angle more yellow, or black, or gray. It was puzzling trying to figure out how she made her color re-blend with each look. The light could also play tricks on you when it shined at a different angle, changing her blending of colors yet again. She just blended into an array of multiple cats, yet she was her own unique member of the feline family.

It was about this time that news seemed to travel and several more cats appeared on our doorstep. The first incident involved two Siamese siblings arriving looking scraggly and thin. A young girl brought them to the door claiming she found them on the street. However after a brief conversation I had with these two I found out that they belonged to the girl and her parents threatened to kill them if she didn't get rid of them. I had my doubts about these two. They were scared of everything, but that didn't seem to affect the decision to welcome them into my home. Sam and Samantha were the names given to them by our humans. When at first Sam and Samantha came into the house they were offered food and water, but their gratefulness was anything but.

"Get away!" screamed Samantha.

"*Maaorrao!*" Sam simply growled while simultaneously shoving as much food as he could into his mouth.

"It's okay, strangers. The humans here give us plenty of food." I attempted to communicate with the newbies, but to no avail.

Finally the humans realized what was happening and thankfully they intervened. Beth was the first one to introduce the "quarantine room." This was simply a separate room in the house with little furniture, and when she was done with it there was even less. The room consisted of a litterbox, some jingle bell balls, a comfy pillow, and two scratching posts. However, the best part was the food and water dishes, which we were all convinced, held special food.

Samantha and Sam found themselves put into the room with the door firmly closed. The rest of us shoved our noses under the door as far as possible and kept breathing in the scent of the newbies. The humans, it seemed, were the only ones who went in and out of the room. When they did it was annoying that quite a bit of time was spent in there. You could hear soft talking and with an occasional voice raised. When the latter happened it usually sounded like a reprimand.

"No." "Get down."

But then at other times I could pick up more gentle and reaffirming tones.

"There you go." "Nice kitty." "Ahh, so sweet, thank you for the kisses."

These were spoken by both of our humans and were very annoying to the rest of us.

"Hey Whitie? Why do *they* get such special attention? Is that how it's done here?" Bear questioned me at length one day.

"It is if I say it is!" I responded offended that Bear would think I had no control over the situation. However, I was secretly annoyed at the entire scene as well.

After about a week of this strange behavior from our humans, the door to the special room opened and Samantha and Sam came out a bit more timid and cooperative. We of course had to do the honorary sniffing and examining of each of them, but this time the brother and sister were more willing to accept and did not try so hard to fight us.

While the newcomers were becoming acclimated to the household, I soon discovered that Sam enjoyed venturing outside with Sweetie and I. Sparkles was still content to stay inside with Trouble and Samantha, but now there was three of us again who went on adventures. We looked like an interesting clan, Bear leading the way. When I allowed him to, of course. Sam darting back and forth across the street, into the woods, back out onto the street again, and then he would do the occasional dash through someone's yard. Sweetie was just happy to be outside of the house. Then there was me of course, The King. Our humans simply thought they were indulging our wild nature by allowing us outside. They did not realize that the outside could be a dangerous place for a cat. It was on such a fateful day, when life would never be the same again.

<<< TWELVE >>>

It started out as any other day of exploration, except Sweetie was a bit more adventurous than usual. He had just enjoyed a bubble bath which Kurt was so used to by now that there were times when my human would indulge Sweetie, with his own bath time. Kurt would put a small amount of water with bubbles into the bathtub and then call for Sweetie, who had already heard the water running in the tub, eagerly awaiting his turn.

I never did understand that cat. I attempted so many times to inform him that cats do not like water, but he was incapable of understanding. He seemed to do his own thing regardless of what cats were supposed to do. Sweetie would splash in that awful water with those bubbles surrounding him, blissfully ignorant to the rules of being a cat. I had actually gotten so used to it by this time, that I would sit on the edge of the tub and occasionally wonder what it might be like. Dismiss that thought for now.

That fateful day we had left Sweetie to play in the tub while Bear, Sam and I went on an adventure. It wasn't long though when Sweetie caught up to us. Sweetie had just come alongside the three of us when he spied sometime in the woods. Sweetie thought it looked like fun and saw it was long, moving swiftly. I caught sight of it out of the corner of my eye and before I could warn Sweetie he ran after it but the run was cut short when the thing reared its ugly head sinking fangs filled with a deadly poison into Sweetie.

"YOWL!" Sweetie let out a blood curling cry of pain running blindly into the woods away from the rest of our clan. I meowed loudly for him to come back but he was darting back and forth in a frantic run. I watched him as he began to move a bit slower but then Sweetie did the oddest thing. He simply fell down face first and his body began to twitch on its own accord. I wanted to go after him but the snake was still there and I knew better than to cross his path. Which is exactly what I would have to do to get to Sweetie. Instead I elected to go back to the house after summoning and warning the other two not to approach that deadly snake. The now three of us ran back on the front porch but the car was gone from the driveway and there were no sounds of any humans in the house to open the door. Having no other alternative we sat on the porch and patiently waited for the owners to come home. It was already dark when headlights from the car pulled into the driveway illuminating the porch and the three panicky cats sitting there waiting. Kurt was first to arrive up the stairs and spot us.

"Well what are you doing out?" he asked as he approached us with plastic bags hanging from both arms.

"Who are you talking to?" Beth shouted from the back of the car where she too was pulling out plastic bags. That meant they went shopping and surely bought us treats. I wondered if Sweetie was going to come for treats but had already given up hope of him returning when his cries of pain had slowly faded away into silence.

Kurt opened the door and Sam and Bear ran in, but I held back trying to get Kurt to understand that Sweetie was out there, probably hurt if not worse. Kurt pushed me inside, but even then, I balked at the unspoken command. Sweetie was out there, hurt and of course the large bird of prey was circling in the area where I had last seen Sweetie. I could no longer smell the snake so I had assumed he had slithered off to find another victim, that devil.

I kept running to the front door trying to get their attention to go look at Sweetie. I could feel in my cat soul that he was fading away fast. Humans don't understand how a cat can feel. They call it instinct but it is much more. We can feel when our humans are sad and we will offer comfort in the form of a head butt. The feeling of pain from another feline is also transferred to all felines in the clan. When that occurs we will offer comfort, which is what Sweetie needed at the moment.

Finally Beth opened the door and I flew out paws barely touching the steps as I leaped off the porch and ran in the direction I had last seen Sweetie. When I got to him he was taking his last breaths. His body was rigid and he had swollen up so badly his skin was breaking open with an oozing substance dripping out onto the leaves making them turn a brownish color. I heard more birds of prey above, they were circling, waiting for Sweetie's last breath so they could begin their feast. I couldn't imagine why our humans weren't here, helping him. I would have even considered encouraging Sweetie to enter the litter-less box as a last chance to possibly live. But I knew deep down that was no longer an option and besides, the litter-less box reeked of death or destruction when it came to the feline community.

"Sweetie," I communicated to him as only cats can do. "It's okay if you want to let go. Rest Sweetie. You crazy water loving cat."

With the word water, Sweetie opened his eyes and gazed at me and with his last breath he said, "But cats aren't supposed to love water, but I do."

With that said, Sweetie passed over to the Rainbow Bridge. I was glad to see him move on. He was in such pain when I was finally able to get back to him that the passing onto the Rainbow Bridge would alleviate him of the horrific pain he was in. I knew this was the only way to relieve his agony. Even if he had gone into the litter-less box the end result would have been the same and I may not have been there to help him move forward.

Humans will never understand the Rainbow Bridge just as they cannot understand the merging of cat souls. Oh they often refer to it but only animals truly understand the concept. I think the idea of a place where loved and treasured pets go, help humans to come to grip with the deep loss of a beloved pet. They often comfort themselves in the concept of a beautiful place where they will again meet up with their pets. However the Rainbow Bridge is much more than that.

The Rainbow Bridge is beyond comprehension for humans. Only animals can understand this place and what it holds. It is an unspoken finality, among the animals in this life on earth. When an animal, whether they are loved, abused, or even wild, dies, their soul lives on although their body is left here on this earth. They are given a new body to inhabit their soul. A body that looks identical to their earthly one, but instead this feline image is made whole again.

The Rainbow Bridge has a never ending supply of food, water, treats and most of all for Sweetie, bubbles and bath water, where he could play forever. No more would he be lifted from the human's tub long before he was ready, and forced to wait for the humans while they took their turn using it.

For a fleeting second, I wondered if Sweetie perhaps would become a cat who would have an aversion to water on the other side of the Rainbow Bridge. I wondered if he would finally exhibit normal feline behavior. But just as quickly I dismissed that thought, Sweetie wasn't the average feline in any aspect. I imagined him at this very moment, as his earthly body was beginning to change shape into a rigid stance, his legs jutting out at obtusely contorted angels. Perhaps he had already jumped into a tub filled with scented bubbles and was splashing in the water much to the amusement of other cats nearby.

Yes, I decided that is probably the first thing Sweetie did when he crossed the bridge. I couldn't fathom how there would be a tub filled with bubbles and water there, but perhaps, there may be some other cats who enjoyed that as well. I wondered if maybe someday I would try it myself. What an awful thought.

The birds of prey were swooping closer, sniffing out their next meal. I knew I needed to leave Sweetie now and return home. He would no longer be joining our adventures but would instead be on his own adventure, which I was sure included water and bubbles. His pain was gone now. Sweetie had taught us an important lesson in outside exploring, avoid snakes, always. We would heed his lesson and would make sure to steer clear of snakes. Sweetie had given his life to teach us about the devil snake.

I licked his ears one more time, a final ritual cleaning, as only cats can do, and sauntered slowly back home. Sweetie would be fine now. I was comforted in the knowledge that I had been there with him when he took his last breath. I had encouraged him to cross the Rainbow Bridge, and wondered if when it was my time, as all animals must do one day, if I too would experience that encouragement. I wanted it to come from Kurt and not one of my clan. Kurt was my soul mate and when it came time for me to cross the bridge I wanted him to be there telling me it was okay to leave. With that thought in mind I headed home casting a last glance at Sweetie.

I slowly climbed the front porch steps and sat under the reflection of the light, casting a long shadow of a grieving cat who had just lost a good friend. I did not have to sit there long, when the door opened and Kurt peeked out looking strangely at me.

"There you are Whitie. Where have you been?" His words did little to ease the pain I was suffering. "Well, come on in." Kurt seemed a bit perplexed as to why I was sitting there waiting. "Come on."

I drew my body into the house and Kurt continued to look outside gazing at something, but unable to tell what it was he was looking for. I knew what it was. He felt it, Sweetie.

The humans were engrossed in the nightly rituals, which included making sure our litter boxes were in pristine condition and filling our food and water dishes for the night. Somehow, I was not interested in following them around as I usually do most nights, and when it came time for the riding of the food cart, I simply did not share an interest in it. Now that drew the attention of my humans.

The riding of the food cart was something I began as a kitten. The dry cat food was kept in a large, rolling, enclosed container. I would jump on top of it and proudly sit, my tail at attention, and my neck extended to the upmost position. Kurt would pull the food container across the house and announce for all those in attendance the same words each time. "Come on Whitie. Protect me from hostile kitty cat territory."

I knew this really meant, "Ride the food container so you can show everyone your trick of staying on top and preventing any other cat from jumping on and riding." This of course was my own interpretation but I allowed my human to think he was actually communicating something else. It made him feel good, I could tell. But tonight I had no desire to do the food cart run and my lack of participation did not go unnoticed.

"Hey Beth, I think something's wrong with Whitie. He doesn't want to ride the food cart."

"I don't know," came Beth's response from the laundry room as she was filling the washer with dirty clothes. While she might think that was something humans do, it really wasn't that at all. It was purely for me. I so enjoyed the vibrations. I loved to ride the washing machine while it was going, but tonight that held no interest for me either.

I sauntered past Bear and Trouble busy cleaning themselves and while Bear glanced my direction Trouble seemed oblivious. Sparkles, on the other hand, brushed up against me. I think she knew instinctively about Sweetie before I even told her.

"Sweetie has crossed the Rainbow Bridge." I communicated in cat like mews to Sparkles.

She bowed her head low in reverence of one of the clan being gone. "She is happy now." Sparkles responded.

I curled up in a corner of the living room, unable to do much more at the moment. Kurt found me there, about an hour later, and seemed to sense my mood. He sat on the floor with me for a long time, stroking my slick fur, which comforted me somewhat. His gentle voice as he loved on me made me even more convinced that when it was my time to cross the bridge he was the only one I wanted to be with. That time would be a long way off though and I still had more training to do. There would be more felines to come. But Sweetie was one of the special ones I would never forget.

I wondered if Grey was there waiting for him when he arrived. I remembered Grey and how Beth had cried when the litter-less box still smelled of his scent. I still couldn't understand why the shrill ringing of the phone had made Beth scream that day. Her words reverberated and swam in my head right now. "He's dead! Grey is dead!"

I wondered if Beth would do the same when she found Sweetie. But when would that actually be? So far they had not even noticed Sweetie was missing, until I heard Kurt in the bathroom call out, "Hey, this is odd. No Sweetie," as he began to fill the tub with bubbles.

The two of them stood looking at me as if asking me to reveal where Sweetie was. I could only go to the door again, which did not result in communicating where Sweetie lay. Somehow I needed to let them know.

Beth simply went to the door and asked, "Do you want out again? You just came in."

She opened the door and I stood there gazing at her, imploring her to come look at where Sweetie was. I refused to go out, I knew it was too late and I simply could not bear to look at those birds feasting on my friend. Eventually Beth shut the door and I heard the turn of the deadbolt lock which meant that outside adventure time was over. I sauntered back to the spot I had chosen earlier in the living room and continued grieving for Sweetie. I knew from nature that the birds of prey were there, enjoying the fresh meal, as the natural order of things called for. It simply was meant to be. Animals understood more than humans this ancient way of life. One gave itself for others that is just the way we knew. This time though it was different, this one was my companion. I suddenly found my eyes were wet.

Was I crying? This was new trick for me. Kurt stood there another moment looking at me, with an incredible look on his face. Did he see my tears? I'm sure he did but was at a loss as to what to do.

Later that evening as Kurt was getting into the tub he asked about Sweetie again. "Hey have you seen Sweetie. This is really weird he isn't fighting me for the bubble bath."

Suddenly Beth began to search the house, but I knew it was now too late. She looked in every room, even opening the closet doors and searching through them, the search continued with her mood becoming more frantic, as it became apparent that Sweetie was not in the house. Eventually Kurt joined in the search, but I knew their efforts would be in vain. Sweetie was having his own never-ending bubble bath and I was sure Grey was looking at him with an astounded look on his face, wondering where I had gone wrong in training him about the behavior of cats.

The search for Sweetie ended later that night with Kurt and Beth both walking up and down the street shining flashlights in yards and sections of woods. They never saw the birds of prey as they continued to swoop down and devour his body. There would be no evidence by the time morning came and Sweetie's body would rest there forever while his spirit enjoyed all that animals were meant to enjoy, forever.

An hour went by and eventually the humans came inside with puzzled looks on their faces. They both slept fitfully. Several times during the night, first Beth, and then Kurt, would get up, open the front door and call for Sweetie. Each time they did that I knew it was useless, the Sweetie my humans recognized was now digested in the pits of birds' stomachs providing the energy another species needed to live on. The Sweetie I knew was enjoying his bubble bath at this very moment. I laid my head down and slept with the soul of Sweetie beside me, telling me that he was content and to not fret about him anymore. It was with that thought that awoke me the next morning for what I knew needed to be done.

<<< THIRTEEN >>>

Beth was the first one up the next morning and began walking the streets again, only this time I was her companion at her feet, pressed close to her, whenever possible. When we got near the place where Sweetie's bones were the only thing now left, having been picked clean the previous night by the vultures, I ventured into the woods. There was nothing left of Sweetie to see but some scattered bones and a few stray pieces of flesh, surround by buzzing flies. I knew my human would not want to see this, so I quickly rejoined her attuned to Beth's escalating tension filled mood, mixed with depression.

She called for Sweetie several times and talked to a few other humans we met along the way. One of those pointed to the sky in the direction where Sweetie took his last breath and they both gazed into a cloudless, and now free of birds, sky. The air held a desolate mood not wanting to give the slightest hint of what was now history. I hoped deep down Beth did not find Sweetie's remains, because humans are not able to understand that cats are actually content. We are endowed with a peace humans do not possess, when one of our own leave this world. I painstakingly recalled the days after Grey died and how it had weighed so heavily on Beth's spirit. Finally she seemed to give up any hope of finding Sweetie and slowly walked back home.

The days after Sweetie crossed the Rainbow Bridge were unsettled. I am convinced that somehow Beth instinctively knew what had happened to Sweetie because she never did search for him again. On the other hand, Kurt went out several times performing the same sort of inspection Beth and I had done that first day, in the hope of finding him. However each time he came back he was a bit more confused and even saddened, so he seemed to immerse himself more than usual with the morning chores. Kurt would clean our litter boxes in the morning and Beth would clean them in the evening. Kurt would feed us in the evening and Beth would play the red-dot-of-light game with us every evening, sometimes long after Kurt had fallen asleep. We still ventured outside on our explorations but now it was Bear, Sparkles, and myself, always careful of snakes, reminded of the last lesson Sweetie had taught us. Trouble never adopted the exploring spirit we three had. She preferred to stay indoors and watch from the window. Sparkles often would stay back with her and then it was just Bear and I.

One day I was out exploring and I ventured carefully into the area where I had told Sweetie goodbye. I was not at all surprised when I discover there was no sign of him whatsoever, Sweetie's remains right down to his scent, having left the area. I thought I saw the snake, with the eyes of the devil, staring at me, laughing, as if to say, "I can have you too." But I knew it was just my hyper imagination. After that one time, I decided the best choice was to never explore that place again. It only held sad memories being better left alone.

Bear had already arrived on the front porch as I caught up to him. I was sad and he seemed to sense my mood, so we sat in silence waiting to be left back inside. Neither of us had noticed the car was missing until it pulled into the driveway. Beth was driving and Kurt jumped out, carrying something inside a shirt. They were both at a heightened state of alarm. They simply brushed past Bear and I but we still managed to dart into the house, close on their heels. What were my owners so involved with? I must find out.

"Bear, go find the other cats and tell them we have a mystery here," I made sure Bear knew I was in charge of this strange situation. Lately Bear was challenging my position in the clan and I needed to let him know that would not be tolerated.

"Ok Whitie," Bear responded not for a moment realizing he had just relented to my authority.

I followed the voices coming from the kitchen and saw Beth quickly heating some milk. When I jumped up on the counter to dive in on the unexpected treat, I was instead unceremoniously shooed away. Wait, what was this all about? Wasn't that my succulent treat, a just reward for a day of exploring?

"Get!" Beth shouted at me and brushed me off the counter. Luckily I landed on my feet, otherwise there might have been a huge problem. Oh that's right I forgot, no claws in the front, so I guess there would not have been a problem for Beth. I must find my claws and remedy that situation. More than once it has prevented me from scaling a tree, or making more marks on the front door.

Apparently the delicious aroma was not for me, still I could try, and I did love milk.

The humans had not even noticed that all of the cats were now gathered in the kitchen anxious to understand this odd event. I soon discovered the source of human's rudeness to me. A kitten, even worse looking than when Bear and Trouble arrived, was the complication here. This one, obviously, was not going to survive. Even cats know when one of their own kind is too sick and weak to make it. So why all the bother?

"Whitie, have our humans gone mad?" Trouble began the questioning frenzy.

"What are they doing?" Sparkles chimed in.

"When do we get some of that milk? I want milk," Bear joined the rest of the chatter.

We decided that in order to get milk we needed to make some noise. We assumed the conflicted, cautious stance with our tails standing straight, ears rotated to the sides, and our front paws slightly off the floor, as we began a chaotic chorus of "MMMMEEEEEWWWWWW!"

"Everyone keep it up ... louder," I instructed. We could not allow the one destined for death to consumer our rightful treat. This was milk, warm milk for heaven's sake and we were the deserving ones.
"MMMMEEEEEWWWWWW! MMMMEEEEEWWWWWW! MMMMEEEEEWWWWWW! MMMMEEEEEWWWWWW! MMMMEEEEEWWWWWW! MMMMEEEEEWWWWWW!"
We went on relentlessly determined to get this warm milk.

Regardless of our begging, Beth began to feed the scrawny feline the warm milk using an eyedropper. He amazingly began to suck on it. I loosened my stance to a more curiously, amazed and jumped back on the counter, this time though I was ignored. The water bottle that sprayed us for such bad behavior, sat there easily within reach of our humans, this time they chose not to use it.

"I didn't think he was going to make it home. I'm shocked he's still alive." Kurt was amazed.

"I know, he's so thin and hot." Beth was more than thrilled that the kitten was still breathing.

"Didn't they realize that cats of this nature aren't able to survive? What's wrong with these humans taking on such sickly felines?" I told the rest of the clan who had taken up better positions on the floor.

In the world of cats, we know when one is going to survive and those that are not going to live a fulfilling life. It's our job to instinctively end the sickly one's life, as opposed to having them suffer needlessly. Why make one suffer, they are better off out of this world. Humans were the complete opposite. Somehow they think it is more humane to make them fight and to keep sickly kittens alive regardless of how painful the entire process is to the kitten with the end result still that same. Felines are unable to express pain in ways that humans can understand. Regardless, of this cat survival fact; humans cannot give up on encouraging cats to live and will resort to stuffing all sorts of foul tasting liquids down their throat in an attempt to make cats live. I will never understand the whole concept.

"We need to get him some better food. I'll go get some kitten formula." Beth finally announced, after the puny one seemingly had his fill of warm milk. Miraculously, I had gotten my nose into the leftovers just long enough to finish off the warm succulent treat. I glanced down at the others, obviously jealous, but I simply had no desire to share. If they wanted some they should have come up and joined me. Not that I would have allowed them to anyway, and I probably would have growled making them retreat. Perhaps I do need to take a look at my lack of sharing someday, today just wouldn't be that day.

Did I need to think about training another new cat? Surely, this one was not going to make it much longer. The Rainbow Bridge was in his immediate future. On the other hand, if, by some slight chance he did survive, and join our crowd, I needed to begin preparing myself to train him on the rules of adapting here. I tentatively crept over to Kurt beginning an inspection of the new critter. I carefully sniffed him over making a most curious discovery. He was not entirely domesticated cat. There was something unusual, an inner sense of wild I encountered, yet I was not exactly sure what this meant. Perhaps my nose was still fixated on the warm milk and I had made a mistake in my examination. This kitten had unusual stripes mixed with freckle-like spots on his face. He wasn't the usual looking feline. I backed away unsure if I was performing an examination of this kitten in the right manner. I instantly sensed he was not scared and his nature appeared to be more of a fighter, than a potential clan member.

What were my humans getting mixed up with? I jumped off the counter and went in search of my own clan, who had somehow disappeared. I found Bear first informing him of the newcomer but he seemed more occupied with stretching out to take a nap.

"Hey Bear, you lazy no good..." I didn't even finish telling him off before he closed his eyes and rolled back down to finish snoozing.

Trouble and Sparkles were next on my list to inform. It took almost no time at all before I ran into them. I scrunched up my nose with what I saw. They were giving each other a thorough cleaning, again. Didn't these two ever tire of the grooming ritual?

"Did you see the newbie our humans brought home?" I began my questioning, determined to break up the cleaning session by questioning them. Neither seemed interested in anything more than licking the other's head, taking turns to make sure each other reeked of saliva.

With that image forcing its way into my head, I decided the best thing I could do was to take my own overdue nap. I curled up in a spot of warm sunlight on the floor and closed my eyes. Even sleeping did not calm my strange nagging feeling of a new kitten in the house. It was almost an internal sense, similar to the one I had when Sweetie was dying.

During the next several days I attempted to steer clear of the new kitten, who despite the odds of him surviving, appeared to actually be growing and making huge strides at a pace that was much faster than Bear and Trouble did at the same age. Although the new kitten needed to be feed every couple of hours, neither of my humans seemed to mind the routine. Kurt appeared to be taking more care of this new feline than Beth, which was beginning to make me jealous. I would paw at him, trying to jump in between him and the kitten while he was feeding him, but that only earned me a quick swat down. When that happened I tried again, but ended up on the floor each and every time. Eventually I began to resent the kitten and his time spent with my human.

It was during one of these episodes (me jumping and Kurt swatting) that I discovered the new kitten had a name. Diamond. The ritual of naming meant the feline was staying. It also appeared that my owners were getting a bit more intelligent at naming us too. Well I was still "The King" and I would not be put in second place, not from any of the established felines in the house and especially not from this new kitten, this Diamond. Yet, I couldn't help but feel that this was not a usual kitten. He was somehow different which made me even more curious.

Diamond began to get grow much larger than most kittens and as he grew, my humans began to get more and more concerned. His days of being feed from an eyedropper were over and he was now eating at the food dish with the rest of us. But his insatiable hunger was more than a usual cat. He often looked out of the corner of his eyes, as if claiming a stake at the food dish, daring us to eat too. His back legs didn't seem to stop growing and he often prowled around the house as if he had to hunt for his food. He didn't seem interested in playing the game, red-dot-of-light and would stare at us when we did play as if saying, "You are so juvenile."

His lack of communication with the rest of us was annoying. We meowed, mewed, and purred. In turn Diamond snarled, growled, and burped. Not at all like the familiar conversations we were used to having. The tension began to build in the house until one day our humans took notice and that was when things began to change for Diamond.

Our humans had been discussing Diamond and how different he was. He not only didn't play, but he had become much larger than any of us. His back legs were unusually long causing him to be a bit slumped forward and downward, and his spots on his face had become more pronounced, while his stripes seemed to go in different directions depending on the location they were on his body. He prowled around most nights and slept most days. But his love for the humans was so intense that they couldn't help but lather him with attention. I had overcome my jealously and Kurt still considered me The King of the house. I still rode the food cart each night.

The litter-less box had been brought out and much to their dismay, Diamond did not fit into it. At a loss they finally put him in a large plastic tub with a lid. Holes were put in for air and hoisting it in the air, Kurt carried the tub outside and into the car while Beth followed behind and positioned herself into the driver's seat. She backed the car out of the driveway, leaving us

74

cats home alone. The litter-less box was left on the table in their haste to leave so I decided to examine it closer. I refused to climb inside but I still could do an expert sniffing job of it. In the end I determined that Diamond would be back since the litter-less box was here, yet he was gone. Perhaps Diamond was going to another home with different humans. I actually found myself missing Diamond now that he wasn't here, despite the fact he was so different than a usual cat.

I longed for him to be here now. Why was I so distant to him? Sparkles, Trouble and Bear sensed my frustration so they curled up against me, striving to comfort me. They had already made friends with Diamond so they didn't understand my disappointment in him, and to tell you the truth right now, neither did I. So we waited. Would Diamond be back with the humans? Time could only tell. I walked over to the couch that sat in front of the window overlooking the porch and thought I saw Sweetie and Grey strolling down the road. I blinked knowing I couldn't have possibly seen that, they were on the other side of the Rainbow Bridge and animals don't come back to visit those of us on this side, left to await our turn. Did that mean it was my turn soon? Was I seeing the spirits of those who would meet me and take me across the bridge? Maybe Diamond was somehow brought here to comfort Kurt and it was soon my time to go. With that thought I closed my eyes, suddenly tired of thinking and drifted off to sleep. Meanwhile Diamond was going through a rather unique examination that would turn up something even stranger than seeing spirits.

<<< FOURTEEN >>>

The shadows of the evening began to ripple across the living room floor when I was opening my eyes. The other felines were at the feeding dish so I joined, wondering why our humans had not come home yet. There were times when the humans would be out late, but that was so infrequent that I couldn't remember the last time that actually happened, and usually when it did they always came with treats for us, be it in the form of a new food or other treasures.

Recently, Kurt would come home with some succulent lunch meat. This usually occurred the same time they would tote in bags of litter and large bags of cat food. This didn't happen more than about once a month, but when it did Beth would usually spend so much time in the kitchen, sorting food, opening cupboards, and talking about the refrigerator and how she needed to clean it. I would be happy to help her clean it, especially since that job usually entailed throwing food that smelled heavenly into the trash can. I had since learned that knocking over the trash can held a less than desirable ending, so I decided to give that idea up for now.

But when Kurt came in the door, he would more often than not, take out some grand tasting pieces of lunchmeat, then we would have a feast. Kurt would make sure that each of us got our fair share, but when it came to me, he always seemed to give me just a bit more than the others would receive. Why not? I was The King so I rightfully deserved more.

Perhaps that was what was taking them so long. Kurt was picking out some special lunchmeat and I would soon bask in the pleasure of my treat. However, it did not make much sense that Diamond was with them as they never needed any cat before to do that chore.

"I'm hungry" Bear came up next to me.

"There's plenty of food in the dish" I informed him.

Bear went back to the dish and sniffed in disdain. I too agreed with his evaluation of the entire situation as we had had that same food now for the past two days, and it was long past time for our humans to give us a different taste. Cats enjoy the sampling of different flavors and I could not understand why humans thought we liked to eat the same food every day. I loved it when they would put a new flavor of food in our dish. Sometimes it was fishy smelling, while at other times I got the whiff of chicken or beef. But this food had been here since yesterday and I longed for a new experience in the tasting department of my life.

I resumed my window seat on the top of the couch and starred out into what was now an overlying of darkness. I watched as several squirrels raced down the road toward the woods where Sweetie's bones were now dusting the earth. I wondered if squirrels ever came into contact with that devil of a snake but quickly dismissed the idea when Trouble joined me on my couch perch.

"Where did our humans go?" She questioned in her usual whinny pitched voice.

"I don't know" I tried to comfort her with rubbing my head on her side.

"I'm scared" she confessed.

"Scared?" Trouble was always frightened of some situation.

"Yes, scared. I don't want to live here alone" Trouble began to quiver with her last statement.

I didn't know how to comfort her anymore so I jumped down and allowed Bear who had now joined us to deal with Trouble. Perhaps he could soothe her. Lately, Trouble had been having some issues with eating. She would woof down her food and several minutes later it would all come back up. Of course we all ran over to see if it tasted any better the second time but it really didn't, still we would make sure every single time she did that. When the humans were home this usually drew much unwanted attention from them. Kurt would shoo us away while he cleaned it up with paper towels or Beth would use the spray bottle to make us go skittering as far as we could. Then whichever human found the mess would clean it up and Trouble would go and lie down again until her stomach would stop aching. I could feel the ache in her sometimes before she did. Frequently, I could feel another's pain before they did, instinct gave me that gift I suppose.

I had been able to feel it with Gray and then again with Sweetie. Each time that happened, something terrible eventually followed. I hated it, that ability to feel another's hurt but try as hard as I could, I simply could not ignore it, so over time I simply accepted that it was a part of who I was.

Just as I was reflecting over deep thoughts, deeper than most cats should contemplate, the door suddenly burst open and in came Beth and Kurt followed quickly by Diamond who was deposited onto the floor. Diamond strolled over and jumped up on the food counter as if he was privileged to be there. I joined him but not before Kurt had already pulled out the sack containing the lunchmeat and began giving us all samples. I was appalled when Diamond suddenly got a larger chunk than I did.

"Hey you, I'm The King here." I informed him.

He appeared to be listening but his overly long body and shorter front legs simply seemed to say that he acknowledged me but that was about the extent of it. I climbed down from the counter and went over to see what Beth was so engaged with on her computer. I jumped on her lap but she pushed me off. Well that was unacceptable so I jumped on the table and began to walk back and forth, pacing. Why were the humans ignoring us? We had waited so long, it felt like forever, that our humans made us wait and now Kurt was joining Beth in the obvious game of snub your cat. Well I was not going to allow the humans to play this game. I just had to see what they were so engrossed in.

I squeezed my head in between the both of them while they were focused on the computer screen. I saw cats that looked a lot like Diamond. Tentatively I put my paw up to feel the miniature cats but they felt strange and were unable to paw back. If anything, they did not feel like cats at all but more like a smooth surface. Why were they so occupied with these strange cats when there were perfectly fine cats all around them, not to mention we were much better to pet than those odd cats who were consuming their attention? If they wanted to they could also fill up our food dish.

Beth began to get excited so I just sat there on the table hoping to be able to understand the strange behavior. Usually she would squirt me with the spray bottle to get off the table, but right now she did not even appear to notice I was there, so I took advantage of the situation.

"Here it is, a Toyger. A cross between a domesticated cat and a Bengal tiger." Beth was exclaiming. "It grows up to 12 inches tall and can weigh over 25 pounds. Well that sure is going to make the rest of the cats seem small."

"But why would someone just leave a cat this unique, not to mention expensive, in a parking lot?" Kurt replied dumbfounded.

"I don't know but he's ours now," Beth was explaining as if she had just been given an extra special treat.

"Look it says here that they are domesticated and gentle," Kurt continued. "I sure hope The King is ready to lose his spot in the house."

With Kurt referring to me I assumed he wanted me to love on him so I rubbed my head, leaving pheromones all over his beard. I loved that about Kurt more so than Beth. He had hair on his face and lots of it. Beth on the other hand did not have any hair on her face, another aspect about humans that I failed to understand. All I knew was her lack of hair made Beth less of a target for my love scents. I had long ago stopped lifting my tail to leave those stronger scents, but I still had the ability to leave my love using my head, which I now was rubbing furiously on Kurt. He semi-acknowledged I was there but seemed more intent on the computer screen.

Computers couldn't love you the way cats do. I will never understand why humans enjoy that screen so much and tonight they seemed almost engrossed in it. Then to make matters worse and to insult me further, Kurt simply got up, went over to the food counter and picked up Diamond. I watched in horror as he not only loved on Diamond but then allowed him to sit on the table. That was forbidden for the cats, and I had lost track of the many times I had been cursed with the squirt bottle for sitting on the table. Kurt not only allowed Diamond to sit on the table but actually put him on the table, adding insult to my already injured ego.

"Look Diamond," Kurt was pointing to something on the computer screen all the while holding Diamond as if he was the new king. "That is you. See how you look? You're a Toyger."

That was too much. Enough of this attention to another cat and one that didn't even possess the need to communicate much with the rest of us. After all, Diamond hadn't been a part of this clan for long. Why were the humans being so attentive to Diamond suddenly? I was not going to hang around for this anymore. I went to the front door and began to paw at it. I wasn't able to get their attention as quickly ever since my front claws went missing that day I was forced to go into the litter-less box. I remembered waking up wondering not only where I was but why my front paws hurt so much. I remembered the days following, how I had trouble clawing things like I used to until, eventually, I had forgotten about clawing. Lately, I rarely even thought about my lack of claws but suddenly the memory of losing my claws came back with a vengeance. I desired more than anything right now, to frantically lay claws onto that door as I had done when I was a kitten. I would show them that I was better than their computer and even better than Diamond.

Finally Kurt looked over and saw my impatience at the front door.

"Do you want out Whitie?" he asked as he put Diamond down and approached me.

"Of course I want out." I glared in silence at him.

He opened the door and I flew out in a furry of disdain for not only having to wait for them for what felt like eternity today, but also when they finally did get home I was virtually ignored.

I ran up the road and past the woods, reminded for a moment of Sweetie until I came across a house with strange odors wafting from it. I was curious as to what was causing those smells so I began to creep over to investigate and found several humans there, with the smell becoming the strongest near them. They were bent over a pot similar to one that Beth sometimes used to make the wonderful chicken noodle soup. But this didn't smell like any kind of soup. This had a chemical smell of several different ones all at once.

One of the men saw me and staggered over to me. He smelled of combination of tobacco and alcohol mixed together. I wondered for a moment if perhaps he might enjoy some of my loving, but quickly dismissed the idea when I saw his eyes. The pupils resembled pinpoints, I doubted he could actually see me. Besides, the way he staggered made me fearful he might fall on top of me, which I knew would be painful.

I decided that the safest idea would be to venture back home through the woods, even if it meant possibly encountering that demon snake. Staying here was making my nose burn and my eyes water. I was feeling slightly woozy with the smell of the multiple chemicals and the noise of the music playing was too much to endure.

"Why had I been so jealous of Diamond? Kurt really did treat me as The King." I decided on my way back home.

When I got to the door Kurt was already outside looking the direction I had come from. He did not appear to notice me at first and was looking concerned. He was looking in the direction of the house with the loud music, and even worse, horrible smells. I wondered if his mood was from my adventure and the odd people I had encountered, but dismissed the thought just as quickly.

Kurt held the door open for me but this time I allowed him to walk in first, wanting him to know I was still upset about his prior behavior toward me. I made the decision then that I would visit that newfound place again. I loved a good adventure and that was one I would need to explore a bit more. Just as that thought entered, I was sure I felt Grey nuzzle up alongside of me and positive I heard Sweetie beg me not to go. Why were they here again I wondered as I slipped into the house where it appeared that everyone was getting ready for bed now.

<<< FIFTEEN >>>

Diamond was still getting more than a fair amount of attention but even worse he continued to grow larger. The bigger he became, the more I understood that he enjoyed prowling around the house, but neither Kurt nor Beth ever allowed him to go outside. They both seemed to keep a special eye on Diamond especially when the door was opened. Whenever he even ventured toward the open door either Kurt of Beth would quickly thwart the idea of him following us out.

One day Diamond even voiced his frustration, the first communication he had with any of the clan.

"Why do the humans keep me from hunting?" Diamond blurted out one day.

"What did you say?" I was shocked to hear him communicating for the first time.

"So they call you The King. What does that mean?" His tone was rather challenging.

"Because I am The King. I rule the humans. I rule the cats in the clan and I rule the house." I was not going to give up my status.

"Oh," was the short response from Diamond. He seemed to accept my answer and leaped up onto the forbidden table. Diamond seemed to be able to break the rules more and more.

Bear, Sparkles, and I were venturing further into the neighborhood, yet we still seemed to understand the unwritten rules of exactly how far we could venture into others' yards.

We were just coming back from an adventure when another cat bumped into Bear. She was similar in looks to Sweetie, but this cat was in very sad shape. She was limping with a terrible smell and from her, an oozing sticky substance was streaking a path down her left side. None of us were about to lick her wound to help clean because of the risk of infecting our own stomachs. Instead she followed us up the porch steps and sat there whining in pain.

"Errr...yowl...I hurt so much," she was so weak and barely able to cry.

"What happened to you," I ventured the question.

"Errr...yowl," she just replied unable to voice her trouble more than that.

It was almost time for our humans to let us in for the evening. The night was slowly overtaking the neighborhood. The wind was blowing from the right direction so that I could still faintly smell the chemicals coming from the house. The same one I had been so intent on further exploring. I would have today but Bear kept me off the track of going there. Why was I so anxious to sniff out and maybe even taste those rare pungent odors? Although my eyes watered each time I got near there, I still had an unusual desire to allow myself to be lured to that house. I had recently observed many new cars parked there, and sometimes during the night, when I sat on the couch gazing out the window, I would see an odd looking car with red lights flashing slowly go by the mystery house, but it never stopped.

The door opened with Bear and Sparkles bolting in, but I stayed back with the poor hurt female cat. I knew my owners would help her. They always did and of course I was right. Beth starred at the poor helpless little feline and instantly went to her.

"Kurt," Beth immediately called for help.

Almost immediately Kurt was at the door. Both humans managed to very gingerly pick up the hurt cat and move her into the house. I followed along behind, a great desire to know what would happen to her. I felt a compulsion to know that she was safely inside.

"Looks like she's been drug down the road. Look at her side. Are those ribs hanging out?" Beth was seriously concerned.

"Not sure, but she looks pretty bad. I doubt she'll make it till morning." Kurt was carefully feeling her, conducting an exam of ever inch. The cat flinched several times but instinctively knew the humans only meant to help even though it hurt.

Before long both humans had some ointment. The very same kind they had used on me once when I had been silly enough to try and climb a tree without my front claws, resulting in a painful tear of my front leg. Carefully Beth applied some of the ointment as Kurt held the stranger firmly in his arm, while making cooing noises to try and calm her. When they were finished the newly found cat was given one of the special cans of food and put into the small bathroom by herself along with a litter box and a shiny dish filled with fresh cold water.

The door was shut and I could hear Kurt on the other side of it alone with the new cat. I could hear him talking in hushed tones, but could not make out exactly what he was saying. Whatever it was I could felt her calming down, until I was almost sure I heard a small purr escape her lips. I felt a slight stab of jealousy which I instantly swallowed back down. I knew this poor creature needed to feel love, perhaps even for the first time in her life. How could I justify being envious of her. She had probably lived a life of hatred and hurt. She deserved to at least feel love, before crossing the Rainbow Bridge. I knew the way she was hurt she would be crossing the bridge before too long. She would be given the distinction of being the cat with the shortest stay at this special house of caring humans. I padded into the bedroom where Beth was reading a book and jumped up on the bed, rubbing my head against her arm so she would show me some much needed love. She absently petted me without showing much affection but rather a perfunctory petting session.

Eventually, Kurt came to bed and he showed me more love than he had in recent days. I wasn't sure where the rest of the cats were, but for some reason they weren't in the bedroom even though most nights we often vied for spots on the bed once our humans' breathing became slow and deep. Cats are nocturnal creatures. We love roaming at night and taking many naps during the day. But tonight I felt the need to curl up and doze off to sleep in Kurt's arm. His strokes were more affectionate than Beth's had been so I rolled over onto my back for some much needed tummy rubbing.

I wasn't sure how long I had been sleeping when suddenly I awoke to a strange sound outside the window. I crept out of Kurt's arm and jumped down onto the floor, silently moving out of the room and into the hallway. I saw the red lights flashing in the window and jumped up on the couch to see what was happening. Everything was still except for the strobing red light. Looking out the window I quickly found the source of the light, the house up the street. The same house that had the strange man and chemical smells. There were several cars with the flashing red light on top but only one of those was casting a red glow into the living room. I wasn't exactly sure what was happening as cats sometimes have limited intelligence when it comes to matters like that. I knew by the way two men and a woman were being forced to walk with their hands at odd angles behind their backs that this was not something humans enjoyed. My life with humans had taught me some very strange lessons about what they enjoyed, which often was very different from what cats enjoyed. We enjoyed licking our fur while humans enjoyed making their bodies wet. Except for Sweetie, of course, who enjoyed the human method of cleaning. The memory of Sweetie took me away from the flashing lights and what was happening outside at the new adventure house.

I jumped down from the couch walking down another hallway to the small bathroom where the sickly, little female cat was and the most surprising thing greeted me.

She was sniffing at the crack on the bottom of the door and was saying something astounding.

"I'm staying here with you and the rest of the clan. The Rainbow Bridge is far in my future," she whispered under the door.

From the other side, I imagined her lying there with the ointment on her wounds. I could smell that most of the wet food had been devoured and she was refreshed as well as alert. Had she seen the flashing red lights too? I looked from where I had come realizing the lights were no longer visible and strangely they had disappeared. Having nothing else pressing to explore now, I chose to stay and communicate through the door with the newest feline of the house.

"What's your name?" I meowed through the narrow opening on the floor.

"What's a name?" she responded with her own softly meowed voice.

"It's what the humans call you. You mean you never had humans call you?" I wondered.

"A long time ago, there was a little girl, who used to play with me. She would say kitty, kitty, kitty over and over again when we played. That was a long time ago. One day she went away with some mean people and after that I had no humans who wanted me." She began to cry again only this time it wasn't a cry of physical pain but of the type of pain a cat only experiences when their human has abandoned them. I knew my human would never inflict pain like that on me but I knew of others who had experienced that and I knew it was a pain a cat never forgot.

"Do you want to be named Kitty-Kitty-Kitty?" I asked.

"No, that's what my human, the little girl, called me. She was nice. I'm tired I want to sleep." She finished.

I heard her sigh and lay down and eventually her breathing became steady and long, the sound of an exhausted sleep. I knew she was asleep, so I decided to go get something to eat. When I got to the food dish, Diamond was already there, but he seemed to be eating a bit slower than usual. I looked at him wondering why he wasn't eating like he normally did when I saw that slight glimmer in his eye. He was prowling again. Sometimes he would prowl while simply eating. It was almost as if he had to hunt his food even though it was freely available. I guess that's what made him happy.

I went back in search of Kurt's arm but Bear and Trouble were already there so instead I curled up at his feet and his deep breathing lulled me back into a contended sleep. The flashing red lights were gone and again the house was quiet. But the chemical smell seemed to seep into the room through the open window. Sometimes it was strong and other times not so much. I would have to go and investigate that chemical smell soon. I simply needed to find out what it was all about. I also decided that I would go on my own, leaving my friends behind. This was an adventure I wanted to be solely mine, and with that thought I went off to dream of catnip and litter boxes.

<<< **SIXTEEN** >>>

Morning seemed to come slower than usual. It was one of those days when the humans didn't have to wake up before the sun was up. I loved those mornings because the humans always seemed less distracted with whatever it was that took them away from the house forever, or at least forever to a cat. Cats cannot tell time like humans. We have no concept of time and only measure days with the rising and setting of the sun, coupled by a few naps in between, and of course eating. I gingerly slid off the bed, and after visiting the litterbox, went to find my new friend. I was sniffing at the bathroom door before the newbie awoke. I could tell she was still asleep by her breathing and the stillness on the other side of the door. Almost silently, she padded over to me and gave me a reassuring sneeze.

"How do you feel today?" I asked more out of curiosity than actual concern.

"Sore, but a bit better." She replied still using that small frail voice.

"The humans are asleep, so in a little while I'm sure they'll come visit you." I tried to make her understand the way it was here. However, I doubted she truly could comprehend.

"What are humans?"

"They are," I wasn't sure how to answer this. "They are the ones I rescue."

"Rescue? Is that what we do?" Kitty-Kitty-Kitty asked.

"Well, yes, of course. We are responsible for making sure they are loved and well taken care of. And of course we wake them up every day so they can feed us and clean our litter and, well, just love on us. That's what we are here for." I was quickly realizing that this wasn't going quite as well as I anticipated. Looking to figure out a way to end this conversation I decided to tell her that I needed to check on my humans so that I could fulfill my duty.

"Look Kitty-Kitty-Kitty," We need to shorten her name I decided to work on that later. "I'm going to make sure the humans are awake, I'll be right back."

"Please hurry back," She seemed to almost breathe straight through the door. "I'm hurting badly again and I don't think I can stay in here much longer."

With that plead; I skittered across the hallway floor and into the bedroom. As I pounced up on Kurt's stomach he gave a quick exhale and opened his eyes with a start.

"Oh Whitie, that one hurt. You big lug!" He seemed annoyed. "What do you want King?"

I tried to communicate with him to get up and go see Kitty-Kitty-Kitty but he did not seem to get the message, so I knew I had to be more forceful. Kurt was attempting to close his eyes again. I looked at Beth and knew she was nowhere near waking up, so I tried a different approach. I turned so that my tail was toward Kurt's face and deliberately sat down. Well this was not going to work any better, when Kurt pushed me away with an even worse groan than before. I sat turned around and began to paw at his nose. Kurt simply turned over so that his back was now facing me as he buried his head in the pillow.

I decided to go and try Beth. She was lying on her side so I slid up and very gently pawed at her face. That got me the push of her hand instead of my desired result. The sun was just beginning to shine through the blinds, so I decided that maybe I would let more of the sun in. I jumped over onto the small table beside the bed and attempted to move the blinds aside to let more sunlight in. Instead of succeeding, I stepped on a black, metal box and a loud sound came from the direction of the television. It sounded almost like the noise a group of cats would make if they all used their scratching posts at the same time, however this did succeed in waking up the humans. They both bolted straight up in bed and Kurt began fumbling for the black box which I was still standing on. It was rather amusing to watch him swishing his hand back and forth trying to locate the thin box all the while I was there protecting it. Finally he was able to retrieve it from under my front paw, muttering something about a bad cat and he began poking it with his finger. I never will quite understand human's fascination with that small device. I'm sure there are much better toys to play with than this one, which didn't even remotely smell like catnip. Ah, humans, they need so much help to be able to function in a cat's world.

I found myself getting bored with this game, of trying to wake up my humans, and decided to go in search of food. After all, it was well over time to eat. Padding into the kitchen I sniffed at the food and decided to wait for fresh to be poured in. Now that my humans were finally awake I was sure it wouldn't be long before they brought new food to my dish. I decided to go put my face back to the rarely used bathroom door and find out more about Kitty-Kitty-Kitty, but upon turning the corner to go down the hallway I was met with a surprise. Kitty-Kitty-Kitty's door was opened and upon further investigation I found her gone.

Fortunately, it didn't take me too long to find her. Beth was examining her side and making cooing sounds. Kitty-Kitty-Kitty seemed to be thoroughly enjoying this and then to make matters worse, Kurt joined in on the careful examination. They both seemed to be amazed that she was still alive, and to be honest, so was I. I had never encountered a feline so badly injured. Sweetie crossed my mind again. Why did I seem so consumed with thoughts of him recently? It was almost as if he was calling to me from the other side of the Rainbow Bridge. I shuttered so loud at the thought, Kurt noticed.

"Hey Whitie. It's ok. We still love you. You are still The King." He encouraged me as he picked me up. "But this poor thing needs our attention too."

He put me down and turned back to the injured one, requiring all of the attention. I sauntered away feeling totally rejected for the first time in my life. I would show them who was boss. I would ignore them and go out on my own adventure, but as I got to the front door I realized it was closed which would force me to go back begging to be let out.

The prospect had just crossed my mind when Kurt suddenly appeared and opened the door. Somehow he knew I wanted out. Only this time he seemed to hesitate letting me out and gave me a stern warning, the first time ever.

"Stay in the yard Whitie." I heard without comprehension.

I darted out as the door opened running for the mystery house despite Kurt's yelling at me as I ran.

"Whitie! Get back here!" I heard him as I totally ignored his insistent yelling.

I ran straight for the mystery house, running into the backyard and was stunned when I realized my nose was burning. The smells were so strong I was forced to back away. What had happened?

The house was quiet, no one seemed to be there. There had always been people, sometimes more, other times just two adults. I also caught an odor of something else though, somehow familiar yet new all at the same time. I put my nose down and allowed the scent to overtake my direction. I circled back behind the mystery house sniffing back and forth until I was able to again catch the scent. It was Kitty-Kitty-Kitty. Her smell was the strongest near a small metal shed. I pushed my way in through a metal door that was partially opened and encountered the oddest thing. There in the middle of the shed was a blanket, some clothing, and a small doll with Kitty-Kitty-Kitty's scent the strongest on the doll. What was this place? Had Kitty-Kitty-Kitty lived here? Was this the place where the little girl had shown her so much love? I needed to bring her here and find out. I clutched the doll in my teeth and was instantly met with a strange taste. This was not an ordinary toy, this toy smelled not only of Kitty-Kitty-Kitty, but also of something stronger. My mouth began to droll and my nose felt on fire. I knew I couldn't take the toy back to her without the intense droll that was quickly covering my mouth and chin. I felt strangely ill, yet not exactly the same type of sick when I ate too much, or tasted something bad. It was a different kind of sickness and my head began to thump. I stumbled out of the metal shed leaving the doll toy behind and concentrated more than I normally had to on getting back to the porch. The place that held comfort for me and most of all where I could find my humans.

It seemed as if it took forever to get there, but finally I hauled myself up onto the last step of the porch and collapsed panting heavily. The door remained closed and my eyes felt heavy so I allowed a nap to take over.

I was not sure how long I had napped when I finally opened my eyes to see Kurt staring down at me very intently. He seemed confused and concerned all at the same time. I drowsily looked up at him and attempted to put Kurt into focus, but my eyes seemed to be having trouble with that simple command. He bent down looking closely at me and I thought he was saying something but I couldn't understand so I simply closed my eyes again. I felt him lift me gently as I fell back asleep again.

It seemed like hours when I finally awoke, only this time much more alert. I was still being carried in Kurt's arms when I suddenly felt the urge to jump and fortunately landed on my feet. I stumbled for a moment to regain my balance and both Kurt and Beth stood staring at me.

"He must have been sound asleep." Kurt said in amazement at my recovery.

"I must eat!" I repeated over and over again, alarmed at my intense hunger and sudden thirst.

I lapped at the water dish until I felt as if I would burst, and then ravished the food dish, pushing aside the other felines, acting as if I couldn't get enough, and quick enough. When I finally came up for air I noticed Kurt and Beth were continuing to stare at me.

"He's acting like he never ate before," awed Beth.

"I know," Kurt commented. "And I haven't even put fresh food in yet this morning."

"Fresh food?" I looked at the other felines.

"Yes," Bear acknowledged. "Our humans were just getting ready to feed us when you came in woofing it down. Move over, some of us want to eat too."

"You mean he hasn't fed us yet?" I was amazed that it was taking so long for them to feed us today.

"They just got out of their nice warm bed." Trouble informed me.

I suddenly noticed that Trouble was so much smaller than the rest of us. Why I had not noticed that before, I wondered. Then I instantly felt bad about hogging the food dish all to myself so I politely moved over to allow the rest of them to share in the food.

"I'll feed them after we come back," Kurt announced.

With that statement I suddenly realized that the new cat, Kitty-Kitty-Kitty was in the litter-less box and she seemed content to be in there. Amazing! I had never seen a cat who was not attempting to get out of the litter-less box before, but she seemed almost happy to be in it.

I watched still amazed as Kurt and Beth quickly shut the door behind them carrying the box and somehow knew the day would not begin with fresh food. I suddenly felt the need to sleep again. Without even finding a comfy spot I put my head down and allowed sleep to take over.

<<< SEVENTEEN >>>

The sound of the door opening woke me up, looking up from the spot in front of the food dish where I had fallen asleep. As I focused I saw a most curious sight. There was the new cat, Kitty-Kitty-Kitty in the litter-less box. She seemed to be feeling better, and come to think of it, so was I. The overwhelming urge to sleep had lifted, so I trotted over to see the new cat. Kurt absently petted my head while he fumbled with opening the litter-less box door and out came the Kitty-Kitty-Kitty with something odd on her side. It appeared to be some type of string, I thought about pulling it, but somehow I knew that would not be acceptable, so I let it go for now. I had time to do that later, if I still wanted.

"No!" Kurt instantly pushed me away from examining the string on her side.

"What was no for? I just wanted to explore?" The reaction was just as I had anticipated but I didn't want to hurt her. I was conducting an examination my eyes pleaded.

The new cat slowly approached the food dish and timidly took a few bites which brought immediate joy from the humans.

"Hey they never cheered over me eating," I warned the new cat in such a voice she immediately withdrew from the dish looking at me with such tearful filled eyes that I wanted to say I was sorry, but I was the King. The King never apologized. Or did he?

Suddenly I remembered the doll toy filled with Kitty-Kitty-Kitty's scent and felt the need to tell her. "I found something today." I attempted at being nice. "You have to come outside to show you."

"I don't want to go outside. I like it in here. The air is fresh and clean. I have food and water, and no one has hit me," she answered.

"Hit you? But I found a doll toy. In a metal shed. And a blanket. It smelled of you." I told her.

"My little girl had a blanket and a doll toy that she used to let me sleep with." She told me. "Could it possibly be the same one? When the people took her away I waited and waited by the blanket and toy for her to come back. But then the mean humans found me and they hurt me so I ran away."

"Why did they hurt you?" I didn't understand.

"They were mean. They smelled bad when they were mean." She began to cry again.

"Hobo are you ok?" Beth asked.

Who is Hobo? I didn't see a new cat. But then Beth came over and picked up Kitty-Kitty-Kitty and called her Hobo. I was getting it now. They had renamed Kitty-Kitty-Kitty but I wondered if she was going to accept that name. Well at least she wasn't named Grey, or even Whitie, so perhaps the humans were getting a bit smarter at this whole naming thing and if Kitty, opps, I mean Hobo didn't want to go see the blanket and toy that would be alright too.

As the days passed, Hobo continue to heal. She also began to gain weight, a considerable amount of weight and her teats began to hang lower and ooze an intoxicating scent that reminded me of being a kitten again. Hobo also seemed to be attracting more and more attention from all of the felines as well as Kurt and Beth. They spent a considerable amount of time one day preparing a special box with a blanket in which they would gently lower Hobo into at night. She didn't seem to mind at all sleeping there while the rest of us still slept on the bed with the humans until one night we heard her wailing. She kept moving back and forth not seeming to be able to get comfortable.

I went over to see what I could do, when suddenly she stood up, and out of all places her butt, there appeared to be a tiny kitten. The kitten was encased in a slippery substance which Hobo instantly began cleaning away from the wee one. She licked and licked until the substance seemed to just fade away and new fur took its place. She repeated this entire process with two more kittens until the four of them laid comfortably together with Hobo purring and gathering the babies to feed at her extended teats.

The humans slept through the entire process but when they woke up the next day they were overcome with amazement. I personally thought it was a bit too much attention for something so small and scraggly, but they both spent more time than I thought was necessary gazing at Hobo and her kittens, eventually ending up with both of the humans rushing out the door and of course forgetting to put fresh food out for us.

Hobo didn't eat that entire first day her kittens were with her and when Kurt came home from work earlier than usual he even put a can of wet food in the box just for Hobo. When I attempted to eat it, he rudely shooed me away. I sulked deciding to deprive Kurt of my attention and went outside on another adventure. Lately, I had to go by myself since oddly Bear and Sparkles seemed less willing to accompany me. I continued to venture to the mystery house but hadn't seen any humans there for quite some time. The chemical smells seemed to be fading away, but there was an area where the odors were still concentrated and anytime I got too close my eyes and nose burned. I knew it was probably bad for me but I felt a compulsion to explore and understand the reason why this was happening.

The metal shed had begun to collapse and one time when I ventured into it with the hope of recovering the blanket and doll toy, I was almost trapped by metal that had fallen when I stepped the wrong way. That time hurt and it was a long time before I ventured back there again. This time though I simply looked into the metal shed and decided against exploring there.

On the way back I glanced over at the woods which long ago held Sweetie's remains but the scent of him was long gone and he no longer seemed to beckon me from the Rainbow Bridge so I could only conclude he was finally content. For a fleeting moment I imagined what it would be like to be reunited with Sweetie and Gray. I missed both of them and felt a longing to go see them. I knew that could never happen though, because once a cat crosses to the other side there was no coming back. So why did I feel their spirit with me at times? I pondered this mystery as I made my way back to the house. I suddenly felt an intense need hoping my human would be in a better mood and give me some loving.

<<< EIGHTEEN >>>

The kittens grew and began to eat at the feeding dish. Hobo's box was taken away and one day she was loaded up into the litter-less box but came home several hours later with a plastic cone on her head. She seemed tired and sore so I didn't bother to talk to her although ever since the kittens were born she only seemed to have time for them. The humans gave them some unique names, Squirt who had white legs and a black body. He was the shortest of all and had a tail that was slightly bent at the end, the unfortunate accident of Beth stepping on it one day.

Then there was Bandit, a long haired black and white cat who had one eye that was slightly closed all the time, making him appear to look at you with suspicion.

Lastly there was an orange stripped cat who was named Ranger. Ranger didn't know when to stop growing and he quickly became almost as large as Diamond, who by now had become the one who challenged me for Kurt's attention. Kurt seemed to dote on him and Diamond often pushed me aside to lay in Kurt's arm at night. Of course that didn't last too long. I had to remind him who was The King.

Our house became known for taking in strays and soon several more joined us. There was a clumped ball of long white fur known as Baby who joined the clan. She was dumped off by a young girl claiming she found her on the side of the road. However, after our initial conversation, I found out she was really the little girl's kitten and she didn't want her anymore.

"Why is she leaving me?" Baby cried out as the little girl walked away.

"Some humans just don't want cats." I attempted to explain the situation to her. Unfortunately, this new cat, Baby, just did not want to accept her new home. "But the humans here love cats and they rescue us," I continued in the most pleading voice I knew as a cat.

"But I love my human." Baby continued to cry.

"You will learn to love the humans here," I assured her.

Baby was not only welcomed into the family, our clan of cats and humans, but she became a favorite of Beth's. Beth seemed to instantly understand that Baby needed special attention and she would hold her and give her so much attention that soon Baby stopped missing her young girl and became attached to Beth. Everywhere Beth went, Baby would follow.

Our clan would continue to grow by several more over the next several months. It was rather odd how humans seemed to know where cats would get love and acceptance, but I worried that too many might be detrimental to our overall clan, combined with the fact that not all cats can live together, which is something else humans fail to recognize. Cats do have feline enemies, and I feared that with each new cat being introduced that perhaps there might be one that was not capable of acceptance by the clan. However, that appeared not to be the case as two more cats were introduced.

Star arrived one day in a most unique manner. He was a large cat, tuxedo in markings but his left eye looked horrible. When he arrived via a human, of course, who no longer wanted him, my owners knew instantly to take him to the vet. They loaded him up in the litter-less box and immediately left. I was astounded to how much attention that he got since it was just an eye problem. I mean cats can live without one eye you know.

We do have other senses that, as cats, we have learned to use much more than humans do. Our sense of touch is in our whiskers and we can located with precise accuracy our every step. We also use our whiskers to love on our mates that we choose. You see humans think, and they are so wrong, that they choose us, when in fact we choose them. Our whiskers enable us to establish many aspects of our surroundings but only one of my humans had whiskers. I enjoyed snuggling up in Kurt's whiskers that seemed to take over his face.

Beth on the other hand had no whiskers at all unless you count those couple of stray ones that she would pluck out of her face with a sharp metal instrument all the while complaining. I didn't understand it all. Cats clean their whiskers, almost revere their whiskers and only one of my humans seemed to even care about theirs. Oh well, I guess that's some of the human side that cats will never truly understand.

Star did not come home with Beth and Kurt but he did appear several days later in a most unique manner. Beth brought him home with her when she came home from work. I had begun to understand that work was the place my humans rushed out the door for on those mornings when life seemed hectic to a cat. Only once did Beth bring cats home and that was the day Trouble and Bear were introduced.

Star seemed a bit distressed and the infected eye he had was no longer there. Instead there were pieces of a stringy substance that when I tried to pull at it sent both of my humans into a frenzy.

"It really doesn't hurt," Star told me the second day he was with us.

"But it looks funny," I couldn't help but reply.

"Well let me show you how funny it can be." He challenged me to a game of wrestle the catnip-filled mouse toy. I decided to be a good sport and allowed him to win the game, even though I knew I could have taken it from his mouth.

Star fit in with the rest of the clan in a way only cats could do. I often heard our owners marvel at the star shaped spot of white fur on his forehead, and realized that perhaps my humans were getting a bit more intelligent at naming us, because this name fit the personality of the cat. Not only did he have a distinct star marking that stood out from the rest of him but he appeared to be a star when it came to the catnip-filled mouse toy. He never lost, not even once. Which began to annoy me slightly. After all I was The King, and I was the one who should always determine who won a game.

I couldn't understand though why I was slowing down. I wasn't so old that my senses were beginning to go as some cats experience in their aging years. I had taken an odd attraction to roaming alone to the strange house up the road and somehow understood not to take the other cats with me. There was just something oddly compelling about the house even more so that now people were there again, but only during the nighttime, I found myself aching in an odd manner to go there and sniff the strange smells that came from inside the house even though sometimes it made me sick, I still continued.

Puter earned his name in a funny kind of way. He came to us one day from a shelter. At least that was the story he gave. Beth received a phone call asking her to come and foster a cat. Foster to the rest of us meant that the cat would be with us a short time, while other humans came and gloated over and played with the foster cats, eventually taking one of them away to a new home. I always assumed that foster cats went on a new adventure with the people who took them away. The foster cats were never at the house for a long time and they never did return, so I really did not get the opportunity to let them know who was boss here, The King. They were usually kept in a separate room and were isolated from us for the most part. The foster cats would receive special food sometimes, and once I had a chance to sneak a taste of it and quickly found out their food wasn't nearly as tasty.

This foster cat though was not put into the special room, but instead was introduced to the rest of us, and it did not take too long to realize how he got his name. One day Kurt was sitting at the table typing away on the computer and I attempted to engage my human in the game where I would swat at the pictures it displayed. I never really did understand the connection between the squares he would hit with his fingers, and the pictures that would appear on the screen. Today I decided instead to focus on sitting in his lap, rubbing against his whiskers, sharing my love.

This did not last too long though when I caught a glimpse of a feline leaping from the floor onto the tray of black and white mini squares.

"Hey!!" Kurt yelled.

"Ah-ha...here they are." Puter was delighted with his find, so of course I had to make sure it was worthy of the attention. As I got into the action Kurt continued to yell.

"Get off! Get Off! Off! Off!"

"BETH!"

Oh I better leave, he's getting reinforcement now. I jumped down and sat looking so innocent.

Beth quickly came and hauled Puter away but not before he managed to snap one of the mini black squares off and landing it right in front of me.

"Now what is this?" I peered at it suddenly interested. I batted it with my paw and was delighted to see that it slid across the floor which was rewarded with my humans scrambling to play too. Puter scarfed it up with his mouth and took off with the humans in hot pursuit.

Thus his name Puter, for his fascination with computer keyboards. Puter began the game and while I had little desire to play it, the humans seemed to be a bit overwhelmed with playing. I was not at all sure either one of them found it fun but Puter sure did.

"Give me that!" Beth dove onto the floor trying to get the toy from Puter who quickly thwarted her attempt.

"NO!" Kurt being the more aggressive one attempted with the same results.

Every time they played this game, the clan just watched from our various positions enjoying the scene.

"Hey everyone," I joined in to communicate that I was having fun. "Let's see what happens here."

"Looks as if the humans are in for a real treat with this new one." Baby commented which had the rest of us staring in confusion as Baby rarely communicates with us.

"Humans will never learn that cats are by far more agile and, well, just better." Bear gloated over the two humans running back and forth, all the while Puter delicately held the prize in his mouth.

Eventually Beth and Kurt gave up, and Puter simply hid the newly found toy under the couch, joined with other jingle bells, catnip-filled mice, and treasures we occasionally found to be useful. We were depriving our humans of the toys as well as demonstrating our need to be in control. I, for one, had a fixation with colorful, elastic bands that Beth would often put in her hair. I discovered that by opening one of the drawers in the bathroom it would yield me this special delight. I loved batting them back and forth on the floor until I was discovered, usually by Beth, and she would take them away from me, place them back in the same drawer where I would await my time, to go back, and grab one again. One time I tried to take one out of her hair, which only gained me a swift swat on the rear end, so I decided right then and there to simply wait until they were put into the drawer again. One time I found one in her purse and quickly latched onto the colorful elastic band flicking it out of her purse to neatly land on the floor where I played most of the day with it until finally hiding it in the couch.

Puter would continue to sneak those squares from the laptop any chance he got. Eventually our owners became more cautious of him and set the spray bottle beside them while they were working. Puter took no time at all in learning about water and while no cat could ever love water as much as Sweetie did, if he felt he could get a treasure off of the computer to hide in the couch, he would risk getting wet for it. However, the underneath of the couch would soon hold a treasure of a different sort.

<<< NINETEEN >>>

Kurt began putting food in a special dish out on the porch because sometimes I would not come in before they left for work, causing me to be left outside all day. He also made sure I had fresh water in a container similar to the big one in the house. The food and water dishes inside the house seemed to grow in size. With more of us there to feed and provide fresh water for our humans came home one day with three much larger containers. One held food and the other two were for our water. While I still rode the food cart and protected Kurt from "hostile kitty cat territory" as he like to call it, the need to fill them each day did not stop because the dish was larger. With all of us now rescuing our humans there was an increasing need for more food.

I was sitting on the porch one day, gazing at the food dish and wondering if I was hungry when a thin cat timidly climbed the stairs. Although I gave her my *'this my territory look,'* I felt that somehow she was there out of desperation. Her story was unique yet reflective of how some humans treat cats badly. Her owners had moved away and simply left her. She was so hungry when she smelled the food that Kurt put out for me that I couldn't help but share with her.

"How long have you gone without eating," I asked as she began to eat so ravenously that I knew she needed the food more than me.

"My humans left a long time ago. They put me outside and I have only eaten some lizards and a small mouse, both of which I had to catch first. They weren't very good but I was so hungry I didn't care. This tastes heavenly." She clued me in on her life as she elaborated in between great gulps of food.

"Come inside with me," I invited her. "When Kurt opens the door just walk on in. You will always have food here."

We didn't have to wait too long and she did take me up on my offer. The door opened and she ran in with me but sometimes being greeted with many strange cats is just too much for one as timid as she was. Kurt was only able to catch a glimpse of her as she ran in and darted first one way and then the other quickly hiding before any of us could determine where she went. We all looked for her, including Beth and Kurt, but it was if she disappeared into thin air. Two days later my humans were still looking for her but I had found already discovered where she had hidden herself by then. I came across her napping one day in the metal frame of the couch where the humans couldn't see her when they looked under the couch. Humans are so simple they only look at the obvious and rarely investigate much further. Cats, however, are always more curious. They will find a place to hide, especially their toys, and then bring out periodically when we wanted to. Which by the way, that was our hiding place for all those toys and of course Puter had some black and white squares hidden there. Just another way cats mystify humans.

At night she would sneak out to eat, drink, and of course use the litter box. The litter boxes seemed to multiply with the number of cats in the house and two of them even had a special motor on them. Those would be the litter boxes not the cats, even though some humans refer to our purring as a motor. These special litter boxes would somehow know when we needed them cleaned. A large rake would scoop our messes and dump them into a container at the end of the box where it would close, thus sealing away our messy litter and making it clean again. This was so much better than waiting for the humans to clean the boxes two times a day. We totally enjoyed these new litter boxes. At first they were a bit scary when we heard the noise each one made, and one seemed to make a louder noise than the other. I found it quite annoying but nevertheless regarded those litter boxes as better, because they not only were clean, but held a special kind of litter that seemed finer and easier to flick covering up our messes.

Humans are such strange creatures. I have watched them use their own litter box even when it appears they are not comfortable with me observing. Then they use water to dispose of their own messes. Cats on the other hand, are made to bury theirs until such a time as our humans remove them for us. We instantly have to check it out though by seeing if there is enough litter to sufficiently bury. It's a cat thing for sure, one that humans will never understand. But this new litter box not only disposed of our messes within minutes but did so with such a noise that often we would shy away from it right after and refuse to use it. Eventually though we did get a bit more used to the noise and accepted it as part of the household routine.

Eventually the new cat came out of hiding and never did reveal where she was. This was fine with the rest of us since it kept our secret hiding place for toys and other items, often which our humans felt were needed, but we instead chose to hide them. Kurt and Beth both decided on her name, Destiny, since it seemed her destiny to be here. She eventually understood it was okay to stop hiding and enjoyed sleeping on Kurt's chest. I didn't mind sharing with her and she would show her appreciation by jumping off and allowing me that spot, where I would gaze at Kurt while he slept wondering if life could get any better.

I still ventured toward the mystery house, but lately it seemed there were more strange humans there during all hours especially at night and the smell was getting stronger again. I saw those cars with red flashing lights once again, however they didn't stay long. Oddly still the next day the humans packed up some boxes and left in a car when the sun was just coming up. I was unwilling to sleep with Kurt that night and instead sat watching out the window. I even saw the large bird of prey a couple of times and his huge eyes seemed to glare at me, daring me to come outside, making me shiver in reluctant anticipation.

The atmosphere in the house was one of contentment. Not one single cat ever questioned my authority although there were those rare moments when Ranger felt the need to advise me about my explorations. He was growing not only in size but in wisdom which I did not want to admit was sound advice. Diamond was still prowling and the other cats had their own personality as well. Some quiet, shy, and timid, while others would take advantage of every opportunity to get into trouble and needed reminding by the water gun to reign in the attitude. I was very much in control and was The King while we were content, living with as a colony of felines, playing with several new towers that were covered in carpet including openings that we could hide in when we wanted to take naps. The litter boxes had all been replaced with the noise making kind that cleaned automatically and once a day the humans would empty the container and put fresh litter in. Life was good until that day.

<<< TWENTY >>>

The day started like any other one, with the humans rushing out the door and leaving the cats behind. We had been eating and sleeping most of the day when there was a sharp cracking sound coming from the bathroom, the one connected to the human's bedroom. I smelled a strong scent of something burning and ran to investigate. There was Baby, looking scared and part of her fur had been singed. Then I saw it, the fire. It was coming from the litter box. Baby was jumping around, looking panicked silently meowing.

"Hurry, follow me," I put my command mode into instant gear.

We both ran from the smoke and heat that was becoming more intense. The entire bathroom was now filled with smoke and fire. The fire moved into the bedroom and began to work its way toward the interior of the house.

Several of the cats were hiding under the couch and I thought perhaps they were trying to save the treasures we had hidden there. Most of us huddled as far away from the fire as we could but it continued. Where were the humans? Why didn't they help us? We began to scream loudly now.

"YOWL! YOWL! YOWL!" over and over again we raged in unison, begging for our humans to help.

The smoke was making it hard to breathe so some of us huddled under the big recliner. There were loud shrilling alarms ringing throughout the house and our ears hurt from the sound. I could not understand what was happening or why Kurt and Beth were not making it stop. My last thoughts as I looked at Diamond, whose tongue was hanging out at an odd angle from his mouth, was of Kurt and then as I closed my eyes I saw Sweetie at the other end of the Rainbow Bridge. I began to move toward him, joining him there.

Where are my humans? Where am I? I slowly opened my eyes to see a strange figure looming over me. This sure did not look like the Rainbow Bridge, and if I was there wasn't Sweetie and Gray supposed to meet me here? This was so confusing, I simply shut my eyes again, the thick throaty feeling overcoming me again. Then I heard him, the voice I would know above all others. Kurt.

Yes, he was here to help me cross to the Rainbow Bridge. I would miss him, but I was happy he was here with me.

"Hey Whitie," yes that was Kurt talking. "Are you ok?" genuine love poured from him.

"I'm not sure," came a strange sounding human. "I think the O2 is doing the trick. Give him a few more minutes on it. Here hold it just like this." Who was that and why was the strange voice at the crossing?

I felt Kurt's gentle, and was that shaking hands, holding me. Suddenly a great gush of air poured into my nose almost to the point of making me queasy. Similar to that time I had tried to eat the worm I found crawling and discovered it had a bitter taste, one I couldn't get out of my mouth. This time though, it was not a worm, Kurt was holding me, forcing the swishing air currents into my face. I opened my eyes wider this time and saw him gazing down at me with something wet in his eyes. Were those tears? My human had never cried before and I could scarcely imagine why he would now. Yet, there it was, tears.

"Hey, I think he's okay. Let's go find the rest." Kurt said as he handed me to another stranger.

I looked around and suddenly saw many strangers here. What was happening? I struggled to get out of the grip of the one holding me, only to find myself unceremoniously dumped into a litter-less box with none other than Bear, Trouble, Diamond, Baby, and Hobo. What was this? I quickly backed up but was too slow as the door firmly shut and found myself cramped in with some of the others. I turned around, which wasn't exactly the easiest thing to do and peered out into the frenzy of movement.

"Hey Whitie, get your butt out of my face," Trouble demanded.

"Sniff it." I retaliated.

She did, so I greeted her with a whiff of my pheromones to which she instantly began sneezing her snot and splattering my body.

"There that'll teach you," I thought out loud.

Beth came over and peered into the litter-less box and we all began meowing to let her know she was a lousy owner keeping us in here. Being in one of these by yourself is bad enough, but having to share it with the rest of the cats was beyond what could ever be considered acceptable by any means.

I struggled to look through the holes in the side and saw not only large trucks with flashing red lights but it appeared the entire neighborhood of humans were assembling in the front yard. Beth kept crying, and trying to get in the front door and every time she did one of the men in the funny looking outfits would force her off the front porch. Finally she appeared to be throwing some kind of temper tantrum, throwing the plastic chairs off the porch; dumping our food dish in the process of it all. Kurt came to calm her down, but she refused to allow him near her. This made me even more frightened. I had never seen them act this way toward each other.

"Help!" We all began to cry. Someone came over and peered into the litter-less box and her breath smelled very similar to the smoke that was in the house. I backed up but was prevented from getting more than an inch away. There were just so many places a cat could hide in here, and the other cats were making it even worse.

" HISSSSSSS, Get away from me," I told the stranger in the most threatening voice I could. It must have worked because she backed away and that was when I saw it. Star was being carried out of the house. He appeared limp and motionless, not moving at all. One of the men wearing one of those funny suits came running over. Somehow Kurt had gotten into the house and came out with Star. Instantly the man in the funny suit put something over Star's face as both my owner and this stranger showed genuine concern.

To the side of the houses, I saw Destiny. She was in the window that was now broken, trying to jump out. Kurt quickly left Star with the man and ran over to gently pick her out of the window and away from the shared glass. He gathered her in his arms. Kurt handed Destiny over to Beth who was able to calm the obviously scared cat, after giving Destiny some kisses.

When I looked back Star had disappeared. Neither Kurt of the funny looking man had him. Perhaps the confusion was too much for him and he had run away. Just as I had that thought there was fur brush against me, no it floated past me, brushing me as it went by. I turned and growled at the other cats who were cramped in this small enclosure but before I could show my anger Diamond interrupted my thoughts with the most astounding comment.

"Star just crossed over," Diamond blurted out.

"What?" I was getting more than irritated now. While this litter-less box was larger than most, it was still too tight for so many cats. Worse yet, it smelled a bit like dog.

"Star just told me. He said he has two good eyes again and he doesn't hurt anymore." Diamond was not going to let this go.

"Diamond, you're crazy," I was about ready to show him who was King here.

"No Whitie, he's not. I felt it too." Hobo chimed in.

"Listen all of you. I just saw Star. He as being held by our human." I wasn't going to let this go, even though I now knew what I had felt a few minutes ago was indeed Star saying goodbye.

"He's happy. He's with Sweetie and Gray and he said to tell you goodbye." Bear joined in now.

This simply was too much. I had to get out of here. Deep down I knew it was true but I didn't want to believe it. Star. Gone.

"I want to go to the Rainbow Bridge," Baby began crying. "I hurt."

"Listen all of you. Our humans need us. Look how upset they are. We can't just go to the Rainbow Bridge when we hurt. We're here to rescue our humans. Don't you get it?" I was more scared than angry, but I couldn't let the clan know that.

I turned and watched as one by one all the cats appeared. They were each grabbed when they came running out of the house. One of the neighborhood humans worked, quickly put them into several litter-less boxes of all shapes and sizes. Ones I had never seen before but this time somehow each one of those boxes seemed more of a rescue than a punishment. The sky was beginning to turn a slightly reddish color now and it seemed to fit the overall mood and blended in with the house, which now had steam rising from it. The fire was out, but so were we. After Destiny was put into the cage, we had run out of room and a fight quickly ensued among us. Apparently humans loved litter-less boxes, because I had not known so many could exist but it appeared that each one held several cats.

Even more unsettling was that Kurt and Beth appeared to be totally unable to figure out what to do with us and most of the other humans from the neighborhood had already left. There was only one truck with the flashing red lights remaining and the men no longer appeared to be concerned about playing with their big water hoses anymore. They had put huge fans in the front door and were busy nailing boards to the broken windows. Beth and Kurt had been allowed back in and they seemed to be carrying out items but the things were dark looking and didn't resemble much of what I knew was a part of our home.

Finally, I recognized one of the litter boxes, the kind that didn't have a motor. We hadn't used this kind of litter box for a long time and I wondered why my humans were playing with it now. Stranger still, Kurt carried out a bag of litter and some food in a bowl. I suddenly realized that it was long past food time and my bladder needed emptied. I refused to allow myself relief in this litter-less box in front of the rest of the clan, but if I didn't relieve myself soon I was going to have an option. Realizing without any litter box at all the prospect of doing my business in here would cause a problem for all of us, so I waited. My owners would know what to do.

Eventually we were carried, litter-less box and all, around to the neighbor's backyard. I had been here plenty of times before on my adventures and knew that the lady didn't appreciate me marking her yard. I did it just for spite though, and with this thought I remembered how much I needed to use the litter box and began to beg in my cat voice to be left out. I promised not to go far, just far enough to have some privacy, and maybe find a drink of cool water.

Before I could get anyone's attention, I realized we were being dumped into the back of Kurt's pickup truck, which oddly enough, was parked in the neighbor's backyard. There was a roof on top of the large back part of the pickup truck. The part with no seats and I noticed it also had windows too, which were gratefully were open. The night air was now settling in and the air was blowing in a bit cooler. I immediately basked in the cool breeze allowing it to wash over my hot, tired body I was in awe of how something so simple could feel so magnificent. I realized the rest of the clan were here as well and there were two litter boxes, the old kind without the motor, as well as a huge bowl of food and another bowl with cold water. I drank thirstily and then joined another cat in the litter box. I no longer cared that another feline was doing the same deed as myself, only that it felt so wonderful to finally get some relief.

I had just begun to cover up my urine when I looked up and saw my humans looking in the large opening in the back. At that same time, I looked around taking count of the cats, and realized that Star was not among the ones here and that Baby had some kind of salve on her burnt spots. She was attending them with long licks and while normally the owners would stop her, they didn't seem to care.

"Where was Star?" I randomly asked any of the cats who were listening, but I knew. Still I needed to show that I was still in control.

"Why are the humans gazing at us with such sadness in their eyes?" I questioned to any cat who would listen. Not a single cat seemed to care though or provide any answers. They were all cowering in spots where it was dark, half purring and half sobbing. I was suddenly scared, more than I could ever remember being.

I crept over to my humans and gave a long purr rubbing on Kurt's hand begging him to pet me. He did with long pets, but there was such a feeling of remorse in his strokes that I backed away, confused.

"Ahh Whitie, my King. It's ok. I thought I had lost you," Kurt nuzzled into me and I finally reciprocated.

I wasn't sure exactly what Kurt had said but I knew the words Whitie and King and with that reassurance I didn't even meow when he closed the back window, effectively shutting us away from what was happening. We could only see out the windows that were blowing a gentle, even cooler, breeze. I performed a quick inspection of the others and helping to reassure each that we had food, water, and litter.

What more did cats need?

They needed humans.

I stretched far enough to be able to look out the large back window and saw our humans get into the car and back away. The house was in darkness and I thought I saw Kurt's face in the window of the car as they backed away. It was the first night I would be without him since I came to live with them. I no longer felt like a King now. Instead I felt all alone. Alone with a bunch of cats trapped in an enclosure. I felt like an insignificant, lonely cat. Several times, the lady with the smoky breath peered into the widows and one time she refilled our water and food dishes but she didn't so much as talk to us or pet us. She even seemed as if she disliked being in charge of the chore.

The moon loomed overhead, a huge full moon tonight. Normally I would have been curled up in Kurt's arm while he watched television or snored the night away. Tonight, though as I gazed out the window, of this confined place I looked over at our house in total darkness and I could just make out the wood covering the front door.

"Why was there wood there?" I wondered. "When were my humans coming back for me?" These questions would go unanswered, as I laid down and tried to get comfortable while the tears began to cover my face.

<<< TWENTY-ONE >>>

Slowly the sun began to heat up the pickup bed, and it was beginning to get hot. Really hot. Raising my head I realized that this was not a dream, and I needed some water. I looked around and there were cats sprawled out lying on almost every inch of the floor. I slowly raised my body and began the trek to the water dish. Puter lifted his head and glared at me as if daring me to step over him. What other choice did I have? I needed water and he was in the way. I paused, stretched, yawned, and decided the best thing I could do was to simply step over him, so that's exactly what I did, much to his sarcastic amusement.

The water tasted a bit warmer than I preferred but it didn't appear as if there was any other water around so I lapped it spilling a bit onto Bear who growled and slashed at me, but I was much quicker than him, causing him to simply strike at the air.

"Take that!" Bear spat at me, spittle coming from his mouth and nose all within the same sneeze. That was enough to get the rest of the clan awake and they all began to get restless making the heat increase, not only from the sun beating down, but from the sudden movement of all the cats.

Wait all of the cats were not there. Where was Star? I dared to ask again. I already knew deep down would be missing. But I thought for sure Baby would be here. Then I faintly remembered, sometime after I had begun dozing off, Beth crawled into the back of the pickup and had gently carried Baby out. Several of the cats had tried to follow her out but she had been successful in blocking their attempts. I remembered it all now. I had been too depressed and exhausted to even try.

I began a dutiful sniff of the area we appeared to be trapped in, and still no scent of either one. Why did they get to run free, and where were our owners? Judging from the angle of the sun, I determined it was far past our feeding time and the one and only litter box definitely needed cleaning, which reminded me of the need to relieve myself. Gingerly, I stepped one foot into the overly used litterbox and attempted to use it. I had barely begun when the realization that I was being starred at by most of the clan stopped me painfully in the middle of relieving myself. I simply had to continue, the pain was too much to handle. How humiliating to have to go in front of everyone. Where was the privacy dome and why didn't the litterbox clean itself? There was no sound of a running motor after I had carefully covered my leavings being sure not to step in another's. This was not going to be tolerated. I needed to voice my disdain of this situation so I took it upon myself to lead a chorus of harsh mewing's.

We began to meow, howl, shriek, chirrups and chatters, resulting in a harsh roar like sound. "Keep it up," I encouraged the clan. "Our humans must hear us."

It seemed to last forever, but really was less than a few minutes when a loud bang hit the side of the truck and the old lady appeared at the back window. "Shut up! That's enough!"

Shut up? What was that all about? So we began a chorus of ruckus again, only to be met with the same response.

"I said that's enough! Now quiet! I'm trying to get some sleep!" She slammed the side of the truck once more, this time with what looked like a large, long, wooden object. Then she mutter something under her breath I heard Kurt say a few times when something went wrong. We sat quiet, actually more scared than quiet. Why were we forced to be here?

I jumped up on top of the food container and managed to look out of the one windows. The air was barely blowing in, and what little air there was, was warmer now. I could just see our house and it had a strange smoke smell to it. There were black marks along the one wall and large flat pieces of wood were still covering the door and windows. A lone bird sat in the tree directly above the house and even he seemed confused about the whole situation. If I was out there I would climb that tree and show the bird who was boss.

But I wasn't out there, I was trapped in here, in the heat, with my clan, and no one was around to help us. A dirty and used litter box that didn't seem to know how to clean itself, warm water, and food that was looking like some ants had found it. They were crawling up from the side of the truck into the screen and down the other side, and into the food dish.

I jumped down and began playing with them which attracted Diamond's attention.

"Hey Whitie, whatcha doing?" Diamond approached me and

between the two of us we starred at the ants as they began crawling back out the screen, each carrying a microscopic bit of food. Ants could be fun, Diamond and I decided, so we took turns swatting them with our paws. It was in the midst of this self-made game we found ourselves in when suddenly the back window was opened and there appeared Kurt and Beth. They still smelled slightly of smoke but were grinning in at us as if we were perhaps the best thing they had ever seen.

I tried to jump out but Kurt quickly shut the door. "Oh no you don't," he said. I frantically pawed at the back window but he was intent on it staying shut. "It's okay King. We found you a place. You don't have to stay in there much longer. I promise."

I wasn't sure exactly what he was saying but I recognized the word King and okay so I knew we would soon be back in our house. I really wouldn't even mind staying in the house and not even going on one of my adventures, if I could only just crawl into Kurt's arm and curl up for a welcomed nap. But that wasn't what was going to happen, I soon discovered.

There was a sudden noise and then the truck lurched forward. We were all pitched back and forth, as we scrabbled for a good foothold, but in the end it was useless.

<<< TWENTY-TWO >>>

During the course of the next several weeks life was even more confusing. To put it simply our lives were down right maddening. Never knowing for sure who was going to feed us, but that wasn't the worse. It was not knowing the place we were living at now. I was grateful that we were together, even though some of the cats did not appreciate that simple fact.

After the pickup truck ride we were carted one by one into a strange house. There were absolutely no familiar smells that I could detect. I attempted to sniff out anything I knew and could place, but thus far there was nothing even remotely familiar, and the feelings of total isolation became almost insufferable.

One day, Beth stopped in and visited with us. She kept talking about a surprise and I wasn't sure what she meant until several minutes later I realized what it was. Baby was back. Beth had left the room for a few moments and had returned with Baby. Although he had cone on his neck, I was elated to see him again.

"Baby, I thought you had left forever. What happened?" I needed details.

"I went to the nice man, Dr. Dave, and he shaved part of my fur off but he made the burns feel so much better. Can you lick me clean please?" Baby pushed his lower back toward me, where a white paste of something creamy had been applied to his bare skin.

I had never cleaned a cat's skin before, only fur and I didn't think this was the time to exactly start. "Uhhh...not right now. I'm so happy you're back with the clan. Why don't you ask another cat to do that for you?" I told him not wanting to hurt his feelings.

Eventually Baby's cone came off and his fur was beginning to sprout in patches. While he still cried at times if he rubbed the sore spots against something, he was healing and I was glad he had not crossed over.

We had the run of only one room with one common litter box, which at least cleaned itself. Then the unfortunate day came when that self-cleaning litter box was taken away and another litter box took its place. When Kurt brought this new litter box he had a serious conversation with the lady who lately had been coming to see us.

She would talk to us and pet us but I missed my humans and tried to avoid her affections. I so wanted to be loved by my human, and here he was, but virtually ignoring me. I rubbed against him, but he continued the conversation which I didn't quite understand. The lady I began to realize was the owner of this new house, and Kurt, seemed a bit strained in his demeanor when he talked to her.

"I don't want to take any chances at your place," Kurt said in an extremely concerned voice.

"Are you sure that was the cause of the fire?" this woman, named Debra, questioned.

"The fire inspector said it was a malfunction, like the motor shorted out. All I know is the area, where the self-cleaning litterbox was, had the most damage. I'm researching it and from what I've come up with we aren't the first ones, but I will make sure we are the last" Kurt replied in a stern tone.

Beth was nowhere to be seen so I could only assume that perhaps this new lady, Debra, was now going to be one of our humans. Debra was all right, but she lacked the affectionate love that Beth radiated on us. When she would feed us or clean our litter box, which was now shared by all the clan, and often stunk so bad I found myself having accidents, she simply performed the duty. There was no love there. I missed Beth and it seemed like forever since I had rubbed against her and shown my love. Even Kurt didn't come to this new house every day, and when he did, he seemed distracted and only petted me as a perfunctory action. I began to fear I had lost both of my humans, and my ability to explore the great outdoors.

I had looked everywhere in this small room and still had not found the door that opened to allow me outside. It was all very confusing to a cat, even one that was The King, and I began to find myself sulking for hours in the same corner of the room. We were trapped in this room with only a few jingle balls to play with, no catnip, and certainly in an area not nearly as big as the house. I was so confused that sometimes I had no desire to eat. I became lethargic and started to lose weight so much that the lady Debra began to notice.

"What's the matter Whitie?" she began to question me one day.

When the Debra came in, about twice a day, there was no darting out that door to see if perhaps it might lead to some grand adventure. She was slick. Quickly shutting it behind her, thus keeping us all in here; a sort of prison. I continued my decent and began to mope around, deliberating choosing to take more naps, ignoring the rest of the clan, even when they came to me asking for guidance, in understanding the new situation.

"Whitie? Whitie?" Trouble approached me one afternoon.

"Go away." I mumbled and rolled back over to sleep.

"Hey, where did our owners go?" she continued pestering me.

"I don't know. Now go away." I was more than surly instantly regretting being so. After all Trouble hadn't put us here. Had she? No, she couldn't have. But why had Kurt and Beth brought us here. Were they ever coming back? I thought as I rolled back over to sleep and dream of adventures at the strange house, or sleeping in Kurt's arms, anything but being here.

"I'm scared." Hobo began to cry as the others attempted to comfort her. I gazed over through hooded eyes wishing I could go help and comfort her. After all it had to be hard on her considering how her first owner had left her in such a state of despair and now, as I made every attempt to not consider the idea, we may live out the rest of our lives here. Why hadn't the fire simply taken me from this life? I could see Sweetie and Gray again at the Rainbow Bridge and at that moment I found myself crying with an intense need to be with both of them right now. I hadn't thought of either of them for so long that the idea of this sent me into a panic. I quickly arose and started pacing the room which seemed to be getting tinier by the minute.

Just as I thought I might lose all sense of normalcy, the door opened slowly at first and there was the smell I had longed for. Kurt stood there looking around. I closed my eyes sure that I was dreaming and when I opened them again he was sitting on the floor in front of me.

"Hey Whitie. How you doing King?" Kurt's voice sounded breathless. "Wanna' go home?"

"Home? Where is home?" I couldn't believe he was here. Where was Beth, I wonder for a fleeting moment? I was so scared of my human leaving me again. How long had we been here in this room? Days? Weeks? I couldn't understand time but I knew it was long, too long.

Kurt picked me up stroking me with long pets. I almost was

afraid to lean into him, fearful he would leave me again. But instead of leaving Kurt stood up with me in his arms. Together we went outside of this room, an almost prison and I found myself for the first time taking a good look at my surroundings.

I hadn't done that since we had arrived on frightening day after the fire. I barely recognized the house we had been in but I did catch sight of the woman who had been taking care of us. Debra had a wistful look on her face, almost one of longing. Did she want us to stay? I found myself feeling a fondness toward her. Why hadn't I allowed myself to accept her during this time away from my humans? Kurt stopped and she reached out and for the first time I nuzzled her hand rubbing my face against her to let her know that while I did belong to Kurt, she would always be welcomed.

"I can't begin to thank you enough." Kurt was talking to Debra.

"I told you it was my pleasure to help out. Where else could you and Beth keep this many cats?" she said.

"I don't know how to repay you." Kurt offered.

"What are friends for? Anytime. I just hope they can rebuild your house. If you need to bring them back don't worry," Debra offered. "I enjoyed the company. This house is too big for just me."

Kurt carried us out one by one back into the pickup bed again. I began to pace nervously that we were going to yet another place and fearful of what might happen. However, my fears began to recede when I recognized the scents of the neighborhood. I stretched as far as I could to the open window, breathing in great gulps of odors I knew was home. But then as we reached the house there it was again, the intense smell of smoke. I huddled back in the far reaches of the truck bed, recalling in vivid details the fire, being stuck in the pickup all night, the mean woman yelling at us. Why didn't I make myself friendlier to Debra when she came in to feed us? I was scared we would be in the yard of the mean woman again. I didn't want to spend any more time in this truck and began mewing loudly when we stopped. I had become so distraught that Kurt came quickly to the back of the truck opening the back door hushing us.

"Hey guys, it's ok. You're home." Kurt tried to reassure us.

"Hi! Oh I missed you." Beth was suddenly there. I hadn't even smelled her until she was upon us. I was so intent on crying out loud.

"They're still upset. Let's get them in and settled," Kurt said. I wasn't sure what the words meant but I trusted my humans enough to allow them to make all the decisions.

Kurt began lifting us two or three at a time, which made us even more anxious. I thought we were at the house but instead we went passed our house which still smelled of smoke and had boards covering the windows and were deposited into a small room in of all places, the neighbor's house. Not the one with the mean woman, but the one that often contained people who would visit but never lived there. I had explored this place several times and often was greeted by two friendly men. I would allow them to pet me but never stayed long enough to show them much love.

This house was redundant of Kurt and Beth's scents so I knew they had been here for at least a few days. There was very little furniture except for the room the cats were in. We had a brand new litter box, new cat toys that smelled heavenly of catnip. Ahh... I had missed this so much. There was a new cat tree that I immediately took my position on at the very top level. I looked over to the one wall and discovered windows that allowed me to see out into the yard which seemed to be a bit overgrown but appeared as if it would make a great adventure. I really must try that as soon as I can. Just one problem, the door to this room was closed. Now why did my humans do that?

Every so often the door would open and in would come another cat or two to be introduced to the new surroundings. There was also a large house perched on top of a scratching post, and the house was covered in carpet. I just had to try it out, so I leaped from my angle of leadership to the roof of the house and then I slid down into the inside conducting a thorough inspection of this newly acquired hiding spot.

I circled around several times and brushed my head up against the inside so that the rest of the clan would know, in no uncertain terms, that this belonged to me and while I would permit other cats to share, this was mine.

I had become so comfortable with my new cat-cave that I hadn't even realized I had fallen asleep until I heard the tantalizing sound of cat food being poured into a container. Suddenly, I had become hungry and I leaped out giving Kurt a scare.

"Whitie! Where were you at?" Kurt called for me as soon as he entered the room.

I wanted to tell him, "In the best place ever. Except lying in your bed in the crook of your arm," but I could only relate this to my human by rubbing up against his legs and letting out a long purr.

"Come here guys," Kurt ignored me and began petting the other cats.

Well that would not be tolerated, I thought to myself as I shoved my way into the forefront of the clan demanding Kurt pay attention to me only.

"Whitie, it's okay." My human attempted to ruffle up my fur. That always got to me when he stroked me in reverse. Why do humans do that when they know it makes a cat go wild? I could only stand it for so long and then I jumped back into my cat-cave where I slithered all the way into the far back corner.

Soon a face peered in and looked at me. I recognized this face but it was covered in soot and smelled redundant of Beth. When the human reached in I realized it was indeed Beth but why did she smell so much like the old house and the fire. I shivered remembering that day and discovered I had physically shrunk back from her loving touch.

"I don't think Whitie likes the smell too much." I heard her say to Kurt. "How much have you been able to clean up and save?" Kurt was now leaving the room talking to Beth but I had managed to sneak out before they shut the door and began to explore the new surroundings.

"Some dishes, a few pieces of clothing, other than that most of it is pretty much gone." I heard the sadness in Beth's voice but wasn't sure why she was so sad. We were together again and that should be enough to make her happy. "I haven't looked in the office yet, maybe there are some pictures and books I can salvage." She finished with a sigh.

"We'll work on it tomorrow. Let's call it a night." Kurt put his arm around Beth as she began to sniffle again.

Does she have a cold? I wondered. Or maybe it's the smoke smell. Why does she smell like smoke and why does she have black streaks on her face? Was she playing in the old house? When were we going back to the old house? Too many questions for one cat to consider, let the humans do that.

Beth went into another room and I heard the distinct sound of water running so I knew she was doing that shower thing that humans are so infatuated with. Cats do not appreciate water the same way humans do, except for Sweetie. But then Sweetie wasn't exactly a normal cat. I had been introduced to the water ritual several times and one time had even resulted in a nasty bite to Kurt's forearm which I immediately regretted doing. Kurt was mine and to inflict pain upon someone who you chose and who loved you was not the way cats were supposed to react. But he simply didn't understand that the water was not appreciated, and then when the stinky soap rubbings started, it was more than any cat should have to handle, so the biting had simply been a reaction. He didn't seem to mind after a few minutes and the bleeding stopped. That was how it was with the humans whom a cat chose.

The love never ended. I wondered at times like this if Sweetie and Gray had found a human on the other side of the Rainbow Bridge to lavish their love on? There had been a cat one time that came to the house so very sick that he hadn't even been given a name. He mysteriously appeared on the front porch, which often was the way some of the cats were dropped off. He had a sickly smell coming from his mouth and when Kurt saw him he immediately put him into the litter-less box and both he and Beth rushed out of the driveway. When they came back, the cat was lying very still in the box, not even attempting to get out. Words like, feline leukemia and very ill, were said between the two of them. The litter-less box had again proved itself to be the container of death. I would never allow myself to be put into that murder trap.

That same night as I gazed out the back window of the house, I saw Kurt digging in the dirt, almost like I do to bury my leavings in the litter box. Except this time the same cat with no name was wrapped in a small blanket and was lowered into the hole. Kurt put dirt over the cat and continued until the hole was completely filled.

The next day, I went out into the backyard and sniffed around where they had put the no-named cat. I could faintly smell the traces of him but since I had not been nose-to-nose with the cat he was an enigma to me. I assumed he had gone onto the Rainbow

Bridge, as all animals do, and was waiting for his chosen one to meet up with him someday. These were the times I wondered if humans really understood what happened to animals when they died.

We wait until our chosen human meets up with us. Sometimes years, other times not so long, often much longer, but regardless we wait. Then one day as we are being taken care of by the Maker of all animals, we see our chosen one. We run to greet them and spend forever in their arms, where time has no end.

<<< TWENTY-THREE >>>

Late that same night, I finally discovered where the humans slept in this strange house. I gingerly climbed up onto the bed that was only several inches off the floor. This was not the usual bed they slept in and every step I took it seemed as if the bed moved in an odd manner. I thought I heard hisses of air pockets under my feet. I wanted to make sure Kurt knew I was there so I crawled on top of his chest and was staring him straight in the face when his eyes opened wide. At first I thought he was going to pet me but instead he did the most curious thing. He rolled off the bed onto the floor in one move and grabbed me up by the scruff of the neck, a fashion that had been done away with since I was taken from my mother. I froze, startled by this sudden motion.

"Sorry Whitie. We can't have you putting holes in the air mattress." He said to me as I was carried back to the room full of cats.

An air mattress? Those were words I had never heard before and made no sense whatsoever. I guess this was going to be my sleeping place now, this room full of cats and cat paraphernalia but no humans. Once the door was shut I was prevented from being with my human, so I sulked. Pacing around the room waking up the other cats, I decided this was unacceptable. I meowed at the door, scratched with my clawless paws, sniffed under the door, and even tried to put a paw under as far as it would reach. Still no response. I could hear Beth and Kurt talking but they were too far away for me to make out any of the words they were saying. Eventually I fell asleep with a paw sticking out from under the door and into the dark hallway. This door was keeping me from my humans, how dare it.

The next morning I awoke to the feel of something brushing against my outstretched paw. I slowly raised my stiff and now sore body dragging my paw back into the prison-like room. No sooner had I done this when Beth's face appeared seconds later peeking out from the other side of the door. She was quicker than I and was in the room, with the door shut before I realized it. She began greeting all of the cats, but I kept my distance from her, convinced she was the reason why Kurt had dumped me back in this room.

Several times she approached me to show her love but each time I refused to allow her. Even when she sat on the floor and played with several of the catnip infested toys, tantalizing me with the thrill of playing, I staunchly refused to be led into the ritual.

Eventually she left and again, was so expert about it I didn't stand a chance of sneaking out with her. I sat on the other side of the door listening to the Kurt and Beth talk.

"I think Whitie is mad." She relayed to Kurt my obvious mood.

"Probably." Kurt responded. "He just doesn't understand that he can't have the run of this house."

"Why don't you go in and play with him? I think he needs that." Beth tried to convince Kurt.

"Go ahead and try that," I thought to myself. "It will do you no good." If I wasn't good enough to sleep in Kurt's arm then he wasn't good enough to play with me, no matter how lonely I was. I would make him suffer for assuming I was a kitten again after last night's scruff of the neck punishment.

"We need to meet the insurance adjuster soon anyways. I'll go in later and spend some time with Whitie." Kurt continued as I heard a heavy door shut, taking his voice away with the slamming of the unknown door.

The house suddenly became deathly still and quiet. No humans could be detected and I was still in a quandary as to where exactly this place was. I knew it was close to my house because I could faintly detect some of the scents. My scent was here of course but so were the other cats' scents as well. I could no longer smell Debra, whose house we had stayed at, and again I found myself regretting not being more willing to allow her to love on me, when I had a chance. Why was I like that? I began contemplating the more cynical questions of a cat's life when suddenly I heard voices again. They were mixed with ones I never heard before and of course my owners as well.

"So how long will it take to restore?" Kurt was heard louder than the rest. When he used this voice it always meant he was the human in control of the situation.

"Three, four months, maybe, provided we don't run into any problems" a strange voice replied.

"So in the meantime we make house payments for a place we can't live in and rent to have a place to live?" Beth sounded upset.

"Well according to our initial report the fire was started by a short in the automatic litter box. Perhaps a lawyer might get you a settlement from the manufacture." There was that stranger's voice again, but this time it sounded like maybe a different stranger. I put my nose to the crack at the bottom of the door, hoping to get an idea of how many strangers there might be wherever there is.

"We'll work on the restoration as quickly as possible," the stranger's voice appeared to be fading away again as Kurt and Beth continued to talk.

Then it went silent again. It seemed like hours before any sound was heard again, and this time from the sound and scent it was my owners with the same sooty, smoky smell like that of the house, when it was on fire. This time it was Kurt who came in looking all blackened again like Beth had the night before. He sat down on the floor, and I decided he might need some love. I was over being upset with him and wanted to assure him that he was still my chosen human. Kurt seemed to idly stroke my fur, his emotions appearing sad and depressed. Why was he covered in soot too?

"Ahh Whitie, I don't think we can save much. We'll have to start all over again" Kurt was again saying foreign words to me. I understood Whitie, but beyond that little else.

What I did understand though, was that he needed my attention to make his spirit feel better. I never did like it when either one of my humans were sad. Some cats really don't care, but I'm not that kind of cat. Eventually I felt his spirit lift just a bit and he began cleaning our only litter box, which I might add, really needed cleaning, and then feed us, providing fresh water, eventually closing the door. Again, barring me from getting to him. Later on I heard the water running and only assumed he was involved with the shower ritual. The house became quiet and darkness had appeared long ago. I gazed out the window wondering when I would be able to go out on an adventure again. The other cats seemed content to be in the room but soon Bear joined me at the window.

"What is it, Whitie?" Bear asked.

"When do you think we will be able to explore again?" I responded in language only cats understand.

"Why? There is something to be said of this nice place. We have food, water, toys filled with catnip, scratching posts, a nice tree, with levels we can play leader. Outside adventures can be dangerous. Look what happened to Sweetie. Did you forget?" Bear responded with some well contemplated logic. Logic that is for a cat.

"I just miss sleeping with the humans. I miss our house where we were allowed to run around in. I miss my life." I began to sound like Kurt felt earlier.

"I don't know." Bear's simple response was enough to end the conversation. He moved on to find a comfortable spot in one of the many soft beds that had recently been introduced to our room. But I sat there gazing out watching the night bugs fly around and then I saw it. The bird of prey as he passed by and swooped down. He seemed to be looking straight at me in the window and then I saw the most amazing thing.

The snake was there in the overgrown grass, but the bird of prey seemed to be tantalizing it as if to say, come on I dare you, and the snake did. He leaped at the bird but the bird was too quick. In an instant, he had the snake by the back of his sleazy neck where he bit the snake into two pieces. The head of the snake went limp instantly but the rest of it continued to thrash back and forth.

I was stunned that such a bird could do that and instantly felt a surge of pride for that bird. The bird had successful killed Sweetie's ultimate enemy. I knew then that Sweetie was avenged. I would never again look at that bird in the same manner again. I watched as the snake's body thrashed less and less, until eventually hanging limp. Then the bird did an even more amazing feat. He grabbed the body in his beak and soared into the pitch black night sky, thus leaving the head to die alone, never to hurt one of the clan again.

Suddenly I was more than weary, I was exhausted. Tip-toeing to the door, I laid down and rested with my paw under the crack, outstretched to that room I had once ventured into. Carefully listening now I heard the deep breathing of my humans sleeping soundly. I was soothed to sleep with that sound and went to my dreamland, where I would encounter Sweetie, and share with him the revenge that the bird of prey had taken on his enemy. Sweetie was ecstatic that no longer would we have to be fearful of the snake on our adventures. What neither Sweetie nor I, knew was that there was a danger far worse than the snake.

<<< TWENTY-FOUR >>>

Eventually we were permitted outside of our room a bit more. However, only when the humans were in the house and even then they seemed to keep a close eye on us. When they weren't with us they would play a special game. The rules went like this: the humans would put as many of us as they could into the room, our part was to escape every time the door opened with more cats unloaded into the room. This game would continue until finally all of the cats were back in the room. I'm not sure why the humans enjoyed this game so much but it was fun for the cats. Cats love to play games.

The days seemed to fly by and little by little we seemed to be adjusting to our surroundings. While some days were quiet, there were other days when we would hear the sound of hammers, motors running at high pitched intervals, and many strange male voices. The voices rarely got close enough to be able to make out the words but when they did either Kurt or Beth was part of the conversation, and then the voices would fade toward the old house again. The scent of smoke was becoming less and less with each passing day. Beth and Kurt seemed happier too and eventually they traded in the small air bed for one that looked almost like the kind they used to sleep on. The day the couch and chair was introduced into the house our door to the small room was opened for good, and we never would play the game of putting cats into the room again. The clan now had the entire house to explore, although I had become used to the small room and preferred to sleep there at night.

Every day it seemed as if more new items were introduced into this new house, but at the same time items that smelled slightly like the old house would be brought in as well. When this happened Beth would take much time and great care in cleaning each item. She would scrub furiously, and sometimes I joined her at the kitchen sink engrossed in watching her take off the blackened soot that coated nick-knacks and sometimes larger items such as dishes. Her mood was odd when this happened. Sometimes Beth was overjoyed and other times she would become very angry. One time she broke down and cried, after throwing a thing that resembled a small animal. She had been scrubbing it and the smell of smoke was strong, when the prized piece broke off in her hands. I somehow sensed this was special to Beth because of the way she talked about saving it. But when it broke she became enraged and threw the item across the room where it shattered against the wall into so many pieces it was no longer recognizable. I felt the instant regret in Beth's soul for doing that but it was too late. I rubbed up against her as she broke down and cried. That was probably the worst day for Beth since the day of the fire.

We had begun to accept this new house with sparse furnishings and a room for the cats when the atmosphere changed drastically. There was a special excitement in the air. The clan wasn't sure what was happening but the humans were filled with happiness and excitement. Unfortunately this change resulted in the cats being confined to our room with the door firmly shut. It had taken the humans some time to put us all in here because every time the door opened to let one or two in, one of us would manage to escape. That should have made our humans frustrated, to say the least, but instead they continued on with their manic bouts of happiness.

Eventually the cats lost the game and the humans won. Which meant we were all confined into the room and soon we heard other human voices joining Beth and Kurt. There was a lot of noise and as we attempted to figure out what was happening. This went on for a long time thoroughly baffling us. We heard an array of thuds and shuffles in the house that would increase in intensity, suddenly ceasing. Then it would start all over again leaving the clan in wonderment of what those crazy humans were doing. Every now and then I was sure I smelled the outside, the smells both strange and familiar all at the same time.

After what seemed like an eternity the door to our room was opened and Kurt grabbed several cats at once and dashed out the door slamming it shut behind him. What kind of game now was he was playing? First Trouble, Sweetie, and Henry left.

Henry was the newest cat, having entered the clan while we were at this new house. Henry was a small sized cat, full grown, grey in color and highly intelligent. He was a Blue Russian breed of cat and Beth fell in love with him from the moment he entered our territory. Henry said very little but when he did, it was of significance. Like one time when our humans were paying very little attention to us and I had begun to brood over the lack of attention. Henry had instantly noticed my mood and called me out on it.

"Hey Whitie. What's wrong?" Henry asked me one day.

"My humans. That's the problem. They are too wrapped out in work and whatever else it is that has them preoccupied lately," I sourly responded.

"Don't you know Whitie? Humans are multidimensional beings. They can't be satisfied with just the basics of life. They need much more than cats do. Cats are here to keep the humans in check. We are here to make sure they don't exhaust themselves before their time." Henry was right on target with his thought process.

"So are you saying Henry, that it's our duty to slow the humans down? Force them to stop, pet us, play with us, and show love to us? That way we are forcing them to slow down." It was making sense to me now. My real duty to my humans was to keep them stable, not the other way around.

"You already knew that Whitie. You're a cat. All cats know that concept. That's why we choose our humans, but humans just think they choose us," Henry finished with such a profound statement that I couldn't argue one bit. That was one of the first conversations I had with Henry and of all the cats I often found myself going to him for intellectual cat dialogue. Of course there was Ranger, who was challenging me more every day. He knew I had a longing for exploration and was upset that I no longer could roam free and explore.

"Whitie, someday your adventures side is going to get you." Ranger would constantly warn me.

"Look Ranger, I was exploring before you were born and I will be exploring long after you are gone." I immediately regretted the last part. To imply to another cat they were going to die and cross over was an unwritten rule in the cat society. Still I found that doing so satisfied a desire in me to make sure Ranger understood the order of life.

The door opened again and Beth grabbed Bear instantly slamming the door. I was beginning to become agitated with this new game. Why wasn't I permitted to play? Baby was the next to leave, followed by Ranger, which probably annoyed me the most. I was going to have to teach him a lesson or two about who was still The King, even if all of this shuffling around seemed to be working on my last nerve.

One by one each of the cats were removed from the special room. I sat there perplexed wondering where they had gone and why I was still there. Perhaps my humans had decided I was the only one needed and that the rest of the clan was dispensable, a concept I had already understood, but simply tolerated, due to the fact the clan gave me something to domineer.

Eventually Kurt came into the room and gave me a most curious look. By now everything had been removed including the litter box which was making me a bit anxious. While you could remove a cat's toys, food, even water, but to take away his litter box, well that was more than a problem. Kurt stood there looking at me. I sensed something more complex was on his mind than the silliness I now been encountering resulting in my being left alone. Beth and Kurt seemed to be in an almost frantic state, with the shuffling in and out of the room, removing first items and then cats until all were gone but me. Solely me. The King. Whitie.

I thought we were going to stare at each other indefinitely. But the silence was broken by his endearing voice. "You ready to go home Whitie?"

Home? What was home? I thought this was home.

<<< TWENTY-FIVE >>>

I couldn't believe my eyes. I was back in my house. The fire was gone, although it did still smell a bit reminisce of smoke and soot. The smell of new wood, paint, and cleaner seemed to overpower the slightly sooty smell though. Instead of carpet there was a slick new floor throughout the house. There was so much room I could run at full speed without knocking anything over. Was the house bigger I pondered? No, not bigger just more space, less stuff, the things humans treasure and collect. That was gone. I began my frantic race back and forth knocking over any of the clan I came into contact with, showing them again that I indeed was The King and that The King was in his castle again.

My frantic assault on whatever I came into contact with seemed to amuse my humans. They not only stood there staring at me but eventually began to laugh. It wasn't a giggle or a chuckle but full blown laughter. The kind that resonates deep in the soul, springing out into the atmosphere I had created. It sounded so good to hear them both laugh. They used to laugh when we played red-dot-of-light game, but that had been so long ago, I had actually forgotten what their laughter sounded like. I made up my mind then and there that I was going to make my humans happy again. Henry was right. It is our duty to make the humans appreciate life. We had been through so much the past several months and we deserved to be happy again.

The laughter subsided about the same time my crazed state of running did, and I settled down to the business of exploring the house. The rooms were the same but there were several differences. For one the litter boxes were a dome style shape with a hood on them. The privacy that provided, was almost more than a cat could endure. I quickly tried the first one I came to. There were a set of steps inside so I ventured up them finding at the top fresh litter. I simply couldn't help myself as I thought out loud, "Now this is a litter box." With a sigh escaping from me.

I had just begun covering up my mess when Puter leaped into the box nearly toppling me over. The litter box may have been larger than the one we had been sharing for the past several months, but it certainly wasn't big enough for two large cats.

"What are you trying to do?" I snapped at Puter.

"It's litter isn't it?" Puter responded, "I have to try it out, but I see you already beat me to it."

"Of course I did." I replied in a haughty tone as I shook the excess litter from my feet, nearly missing Puter who swatted me on my way out. I would show him later, when he was taking one of his naps, exactly what happens to a clan member who tries that trick. Instead for now I decided to back my butt and left a nasty, smelling, toot of butt air on him. "See who's the boss," I finished as I crawled back out to explore some more.

I had just begun when Beth came rushing through the room. She always seemed to be in hyper speed mode. Her hands were full of clothing that was still on hangers as she rammed past me to the bedroom. I decided to follow her in and see if perhaps there was anything that might need my special attention. The bedroom looked the same, sort of, but at the same time it looked different, much like the rest of the house did. The lack of items on shelves, dresser tops, and counters gave the house an empty feeling. I couldn't imagine where all those useless gadgets had gone.

I was in the midst of continuing my exploration of the house when I encountered Ranger. I noticed that Ranger had that determined look of challenge on his face and appeared to be focused on my alpha cat status. This was increasingly bothering me. After all The King always had to be concerned about another taking over his status in the clan, but the method in which Ranger was doing so was odd. Odd for a cat that is. Perhaps now that we were back in the house was the opportune time to have a talk with him about this. I hid until I could successfully sneak up on him, catching him off guard.

"Ranger, hello," I greeted as I leaped from the top of the dresser right down in front of him, arresting him in his tracks. I hadn't realized how big he had become and his shoulders were above mine now but that wouldn't impede me from showing him who was The King.

"Whitie." His gaze was more than questioning, sizing me up almost.

"So now that we're back in our home, you need to recognize who is the boss," I challenged him in a no win catitude.

"Whitie, you will always be the boss. But there may come a

time when you are no longer here. Then I am the natural selection for leader," Ranger said in a matter of fact tone.

"I will always be here." This was something I had never contemplated and now that Ranger had brought the subject up I was alarmed at the prospect of it. I remembered Sweetie and how I had helped him cross over to the Rainbow Bridge with my encouragement to him. How I had whispered in his ear that it was okay to go. Would someone, someday, have to do that for me too? No, it was too much to even consider. But at the same time I understood that cats only have one life and I was determined to make that a long life, so Ranger was just challenging me.

I reared my head higher so that it stood above him as I looked down. "I am going to be here a long, long time Ranger."

"That might be so Whitie, but lately you have been venturing further and further from the house. What happens if you encountered the same deadly viper that Sweetie did?" Ranger seemed to have read my thoughts.

"But Sweetie didn't know about the deadly viper, I do." I countered. "And besides, I saw the bird of prey take revenge on that devil snake, he avenged Sweetie's killer." I finished with something for even Ranger to consider.

"Whitie, there are other dangers out there in the land of your explorations and lately you have been going further and further." Ranger had a point but I was in no mood to let him know.

True, I had managed to escape several times from the last house when the owners, especially Beth, had left the door to our special room open longer than necessary. The rest of the clan was either too busy engrossed with all the playthings, that had been set up to occupy our time, or they simply didn't see a need to explore. From there, I could easily have push the front door open and venture on one of my many and varied trips.

One time in particular, I had been gone for so long and had explored into yards I had never scented before that it took me most of the night to come back. Headlights from cars would illuminate my walk back home but I had become more than a little concerned about finding my way back. I heard Kurt call my names several times during that night, but I eventually became confused and found myself on the porch of the sooty smelling house and resigned myself to sleeping there for the night. The next morning, some men carrying tools and boards found me as I awoke with the strangers starring at me. Kurt eventually came over, as he did most days to check on the progress and was surprised to see me there.

"So there's were you've been." Kurt seemed delighted and concerned to see me. He picked me up and carried me back home, which I didn't mind at all. I had been fitfully sleeping most of the night being reminded of the last time my siblings and I had been forced to sleep on the porch and the large bird had been watching us. The loss of Gray came back to me at that moment with a deep jolt of pain. Gray had died, I would die someday as well. I just wasn't ready to, and I would fight death when my time came. I would continue on, death would not simply sneak up on me, like it had Sweetie and Star. The plastic litter-less crate would not catch me in its ugly death grip. It might other cats, but not me.

I turned back to Ranger now, with more of a catitude than necessary. "My explorations are carefully planned and I'm always back."

"But someday Whitie you might not return. Not that I want something to happen to you, so that I can become boss cat. I don't want that, unless the title is thrust upon me. But you have to understand that someday, if you continue to venture, it will happen." Ranger sauntered away on that short pointed speech, as I stood there trying to decide if I should listen to him or not.

To take his advice would mean the end of my adventures and I wasn't so sure I was ready for that. But at the same time I knew he might be right, and had experienced that worry the night I had to sleep on the porch all alone. But Kurt had found me and I was fine. After all what did Ranger know? He had never been on an adventure. He was probably jealous of my great feats of exploration. Yet, the words he spoke to me lingered throughout my mind the better part of the day making me less than approachable. I sauntered around, my head hanging low with heavy thoughts of the day's conversation with Ranger. Kurt even noticed my mood and remarked to Beth about it.

"I think Whitie misses the house we were renting," he responded about me as I flopped myself down on a familiar yet, different part of the living room floor.

I missed the soft couch and chairs I used to sleep on. Where were they? This room almost seemed empty, much like most of the rest of the house. As the days flew by, more and more items began to appear in the house, first there were dishes which had been lying all over the counter as if Beth had left them just for me to investigate. But that didn't last long as she began putting them into the cupboards that also had the new scent of wood. I had even ventured inside an empty one, when she had left it open for me. Oddly enough, I was able to detect the slight hint of smoke. Of course it didn't take long before Beth found me and quickly swatted me out. I raised my tail at her but she seemed unimpressed with my reaction, so I simply decided to pace back and forth on the counters until she showed me the spray bottle, of which I in no way wanted to tangle with, so I jumped down and went to the door expecting to be let out.

It didn't take long before Kurt saw me and hesitated, an action he had never done before, when it came to letting me out to embark on a new adventure. He seemed to be trying to decide if I should be permitted entrance to the great outdoors or not. I gently lifted a paw to the door, to let him know that was the best choice, and yet he still seemed slow at opening the entrance to the inevitable.

Finally the door was opened and I skittered out leaping off the steps and into the tall grass. Soon my owner would cut the grass and then it wouldn't be near as much fun to hunt in for a while, until it grew back.

Where the road met the grass I began my trek toward the place I most enjoyed exploring. Looking into the woods only momentarily reminded of my previous conversation with Ranger. The spirit of Sweetie seemed stronger than usual today. I quickly dismissed it as my guilt over coming on a little too strongly to Ranger attempted to deter me from my plans. After all he was the most obvious choice if something did happen to me. Ahh. Who was I fooling? Nothing was going to happen to me. I continued on approaching the mystery house. Lately, there had been more movement and I was reminded of Kitty-Kitty's or was it Hobo's owner. Either way, I was reminisce of her cries when she first came, for the girl who had loved her, and had lived here once. I had never known what it was like to lose my owner, and personally I prayed I never would know.

Yes, cats do have a spirit, I can assure you of that. We do know there is a creator who will not only care for us but be there for us when we cross over. There I go again. I was going to have to put Ranger's speech out of my head, it was interfering with my pleasure of the hunt.

I crept slowly and steadily back to where the metal building, which was near collapse, and slid my body in. I dug around for some evidence to take back to Hobo, that her previous owner had no choice in the matter when she left her. Similar to the clan having no choice when the fire had taken over, and we were shifted from house to house, but eventually returning to our home. Home. Yes, I needed to get back, darkness was beginning to fall and I knew dinner would be served and I must ride the food cart. I had almost forgotten about the food cart ritual having been so long out of my original home. Tonight would be the night though, the food cart would be in my control and I would stand proud on it and make Kurt happy I once again would accompany him on his round of filling the dishes with succulent, fresh food.

I squeezed my body out of the metal building wondering why it seemed to have grown smaller since I went in. My original reason for going in there forgotten, when suddenly there was something in my way. I tried to push my way around it but it stood staunchly in my way. It seemed like a large plastic container of some sort, similar to the ones Beth was bringing into the house and taking out soot encrusted items that had been in the house before the fire. Sometimes she would be able to make these items look like new again, and other times she would begin to cry and throw them away. Much like the time she had thrown the small wolf statue after she had scrubbed and scrubbed, only to result in the structure breaking apart in the end.

This container though had a rather strange smell. Not exactly like cat urine but similar to a harsh cleaner, or even perhaps a chemical smell. Actually it was a combination of all three. I tentatively took a sniff and felt instantly sick. I backed away from the strange container but now I was back again in the metal building with seemingly no way to get out unless I squeezed past the container. It was tight but I eventually did it. I thought I had seen a human nearby but the smells from the container were making my eyes water and my stomach felt queasy. I wanted to take a closer look inside the container but decided not to. Getting back to the house was my best bet, but I couldn't help but wonder what was inside the strange smelling container.

There it was again, not my imagination, there was a human and he appeared to be coming toward me. His movements seemed stranger than most humans, I had encountered though, almost a zigzag style of walk. Why would a human walk like that? It was easy getting out of his reach and when I looked back I saw him just staring at me. I headed toward the house and when I topped the steps the odd feelings from the container had pretty much left me.

I scratched on the door, maybe not so much scratched as I still had not found my claws. I usually didn't miss them until such a time as this when they would have come in handy. I really needed to focus someday on finding my claws. Perhaps if I ever went back to the vet, Dr. Dave might be able to help locate them for me and put them back on my paws.

It was only a matter of a minute or two when the door quickly opened and Beth was there. Instead of just opening the door she walked out onto the porch and stared intently at the way I had come. She appeared to be studying the house where the collapsing metal building was, but she didn't say a word until she went in and shut the inside door locking it with a click.

"Those strange people are back," I heard her say to Kurt.

"I don't know. What do you want me to do, call the cops? We can't prove anything," Kurt said in an irritated voice.

"But I think that's where Whitie is going to," Beth seemed concerned and I turned my head hearing my name spoken in that tone of voice. Beth was usually the calmer of the two humans and hearing my name spoken in this manner made me a bit nervous. I hadn't done anything wrong.

"Come on Whitie, let's do the food run," Kurt said ignoring Beth's concern.

I quickly followed Kurt back the hall to the food cart. At least I hadn't missed out on that tonight. On my way back I caught a glimpse of Ranger.

"Whitie, were you exploring again?" Ranger asked me in passing.

"What if I was? What are you going to do about it? I'm The King," I reminded him, but instantly regretted my decision to speak so rudely.

"Enjoy your food cart run Whitie," Ranger said in a soft voice as he turned to await with the rest of the cats at the bowl, which would soon contain fresh morsels of delight.

<<< TWENTY-SIX >>>

The days seemed to fly by and life began to return to normal. We were enjoying the freedom and being back in our home. Our owners had fallen back into a routine we were more accustomed to, which included them again rushing out the door in the mornings and we cats would await their evening return. I somehow knew this had not changed even when we lived at the house where we were confined to one room for most of the time. I often heard their same hurried movements and early morning conversations.

Evenings would consist of the humans eating their meal while we cats would sit at their feet begging for a tasty treat. Sometimes the humans wouldn't eat at home and instead they would come home with the smell of food on their breath. At times I could detect steak, other times pizza, and then there were those burgers that made me envious of humans and wherever it was they hid this delicious food. This happened more on the days when they did not rush out the door early in the morning and leave us home alone. The days they would sleep in and take time to give us cats the special attention we deserved. I loved those days when we would spend more time with them. Even though they were often busy with cleaning the house or doing yard work, or even making the house look more like it used to before the fire.

I took note that Beth had again started focusing outside, digging in the dirt, and playing with the sweet smelling flowers and vegetables, but I found myself less interested in digging in the ground, although there were still times when I would. Which of course would drive Beth crazy. I often did it just to watch the reactions on my humans' faces. Beth would complain and Kurt would laugh and say, "That's Whitie for ya!" I knew he wasn't speaking my name in a bad tone but in one that made reference to the way we belonged together.

I also knew I was getting older, I enjoyed naps more, and while I still continued to go on my adventures, often times being accompanied by Bear and Sparkles. Even Puter had begun to join us once in a while, but often I would return home sore and tired and in need of a nap. I noticed Kurt had begun to look differently at me when I did this, so I tried to sneak in and hide, so he couldn't tell I was exhausted. If Kurt did find me in this physical state, he would feel me all over in a manner that annoyed me. It wasn't exactly a pet but more of an exploration of my body, similar to when I explored the great outdoors. Only his exploration of me made me uncomfortable, so I would force my body to show him there was really no reason for concern, and pretend that I was ready to play, if that was what he wanted.

When I did that Kurt seemed less restless and more his old self. I noticed that since the fire Kurt and Beth spent more time with us. They almost seemed to be making up for the time we were forced to stay in the room, or worse yet that awful night we spent cramped up in the pickup truck behind the lady's house. The lady who yelled at us and scared us. I reminded myself to stay away from her house when I went exploring. She didn't seem as if she would harm me, but I didn't want to take the chance, especially since the night of the fire was still so fresh in my memory.

Life seemed to be getting back on a normal track when one day it changed in such a way I would never look at my life the same way again. It all began with a visitor.

<<< TWENTY-SEVEN >>>

The stranger came to our house one day shortly after Kurt and Beth had gotten home for the evening. I could tell something was up immediately upon their arrival home. Kurt and Beth were both rushed, but not in the usual after work rush session, the one that consisted of taking care of our litter-boxes. Instead they seemed to be setting up for something much more important. I was curious, so I chose not to go for what was becoming, my nightly adventure. I was determined to defy Ranger, and show him he was wrong in his thought process. Although I knew Ranger only had my best intentions, still I couldn't allow one cat to tell me, The King, what to do. I told the clan what to do, not the other way around.

Still Ranger would question me when I came in and often I wanted to admit he might be right. I had become more intent on sniffing the strange smells and each time I allowed myself to do that, the feeling was more out of control. I was used to being the one in control of everything, even my own compulsions. My explorations consisted mainly of the mystery house, which lately had more humans there than ever before, and the strange scents were even more pronounced. I had also observed at times the red and blue lights on top of a car at their house too, but unlike the other times the people remained. I would sit a night on the back of the couch, which thankfully had been replaced with a new and different one than was there before the fire. This one was more comfortable and sat higher so I could look out the window and see much more. I even saw that magnificent bird of prey a few more times before he seemed to disappear. However, there was no sign of the little girl Hobo had talked about, and eventually Hobo stopped missing her seemingly content to stay at our home.

However, this night there was too much commotion going on for even me to consider my nightly adventure. Kurt had become used to me leaving right after the food cart run and then coming back an hour or so later. He almost seemed to accept that simply was a part of me, The King. This night was different and I was about to understand just how different and how humans could affect cats in such a manner that they would never forget.

There was a sudden knock on the front door, something that

rarely happened. Beth ran to greet the stranger and she quickly took hold of not one, not two, but four plastic litter-less boxes. I was so astounded I simply sat there taking it all in. The plastic crates were quickly moved to the floor and opened. I creeped up to sniff at the contents and before I could understand what was happening, the woman who had brought them in was gone. She simply waltzed out the door with just a few words being said. I recognized the word thank you, and call you, but other than that, it was all foreign to me.

There was a cat in each cage, not a kitten but full grown cats. The first cat was an orange colored one with stripes marking his body. I quickly learned his name was Ivan, by the way Kurt and Beth would call for him. He couldn't have cared less though and the more they called for him the further back in the cage he forced himself. This cat was going to be a tough one to teach the ways of this house. That was if he was going to stay.

The next cage contained a beautiful pure-bred ragamuffin breed. His fur was gorgeous and was tricolored with splotches of black, brown, and white. I soon learned his name was Sasha, and unlike Ivan he did venture out to explore. We politely sniffed each other and I learned that he had no front claws just like me.

"I'm hungry," Sasha informed me.

"The food dish is over here. I'll show you," I led him over to our food dish and he immediately began to take great gulps of food.

"Slow down there. There's plenty of food. My owners keep it filled." I tried to convince him to stop, but to no avail. He just continued eating and the conversation was over.

I went back to the plastic litter-less crates and Ivan was still cowering as far to the back as he could squeeze his body. I sniffed the next cage and discovered there was no cat in there, apparently he must have ventured out while I was showing Sasha the food dish.

The fourth and last plastic litter-less box contained perhaps the saddest sight I will ever in my life see. There inside was an old male cat who was crying. Struggling to breath in between sobs.

"Hey this is a nice place, don't cry," I tried my hardest to make him feel welcomed. "These humans are the nicest ever. They take care of our needs, stroke us until we purr, and make sure our food and water dishes are always full. Come on out and see," I tried to console this poor old man.

"Where is my human?" he asked in between sobs. "I can't smell her. I can't see her. She's all I've ever known my entire life. I was a wee kitten when I came to live with her and now she's gone."

I sat there not knowing what to say. I tried to venture inside the plastic crate but realized this was a very large cat and there simply wasn't enough room for both of us, not even my head could fit in there. I caught an orange flash out of the corner of my eye and realized that Ivan had darted out of his litter-less box and was now streaking through the house. I didn't get a chance to see exactly where and besides this large, old cat needed me more than anything right now.

"Come on out," I pleaded. "Just try some of the delicious food."

"I don't want to eat. I want to die," the old cat responded.

"Die?" I was astounded to hear one of my felines declare that word. "Do you mean you want to go to the Rainbow Bridge?" I was so confused now. "But your owner, she will be back."

"No she won't. I heard her say she was getting rid of us. She was tired of cleaning our litter-box and that we were too much trouble. I've been with her for 13 years now. She's all I know. If I can't be with her, then just let me die," he finished with a sigh and simply laid his head down.

I moved away. This was too confusing for even me to even contemplate. How could an owner not want their cat? My owners would never leave any of us. But wait they had left me, yes, that had left all of us, right after the fire. But that was different because they had come back for us. Maybe this old cat's owner would come back for him too. Maybe his house had been on fire and his owner had to leave him just like our owners had to leave us. Sometimes humans have to do things that cats cannot understand. I had to make him understand this.

But suddenly I had another random thought. "Wait. Then they took us to Debra's house," I said aloud to this sad creature.

"Who's Debra?" He couldn't understand what I was trying to communicate.

"She's a kind lady that I was mean to," I suddenly realized I had admitted to making a mistake. "But even when we were there our humans came every day to see us. So owners don't give up on their cats, not even when their house burns down and they can't live in it. Is that what happened? Did your house burn?" I had to know. "Did your house burn?" I asked the old male cat a second time while he sat there crying.

"Burn? What is burn?" he was clearly confused.

"It's what happens when a fire comes and your owners aren't home and then you have to go stay in the back of a pickup at night and…." I could tell that wasn't what had happened before he opened his mouth to tell me the whole story.

"There was no fire as you described it. She simply came home and said, you're all going. I'm done."

"Done? With what? Her cats?" I was clearly confused.

"Yes, done, not wanted."

"Hey there Buddy," Beth gently reached past me and into the cage. She pulled him out even though he resisted. "What's the matter, huh?"

Beth could be one of the kindest humans of all, especially when she thought we were hurting. She would cuddle us, and cover us with warm blankets, let us sleep with her. She would stay up all night sometimes when one of us were sick. I remembered when Bear and Trouble came. She slept on the couch feeding them every couple of hours and eventually she fell asleep with them both wrapped in a warm towel as they slept on her. She wasn't really sleeping soundly and every so often would reach out and feel their breathing, making sure they were alive. This went on for several weeks until finally they were old enough to begin eating bits and pieces of soft cat food, gradually increasing to the same food we ate. Beth was a human who not only cared for us but genuinely loved us. She was showing the same love now to…what was his name again…I think Buddy, she called him.

Beth gently place Buddy at the food dish but he just sat there looking, not even daring to take as much as a sniff of the food. Beth sat on the floor with Buddy and stroked him speaking gently. "It's going to be all right. Come on. I know you're hungry. Eat Buddy. We love you. You're going to stay with us now," she encouraged him.

So the new cat's owner truly did not want them anymore. The way Beth was talking their owner was not coming back for them. Why do humans do that? Hobo's owner left. Baby's owner simply dropped him off one day. I remembered how they had missed their humans and wondered if perhaps, what was his name again? Oh yes, Buddy. If maybe Buddy would eventually forget about his owner too and decide to be happy here. I didn't even mind that I would have to teach him how to be a part of this clan. I just would make sure he would want to live. A cat should never hurt so badly that they want to cross the Rainbow Bridge before it's their natural time.

Beth kept trying, and sadly Buddy simply wanted nothing to do with her. I sauntered over to him and gave another polite sniff, but was greeted with no response whatsoever. It was as if he was so deeply inside of his grief, that he couldn't separate himself from it. I saw the black and white cat, another ragamuffin, apparently a purebred too, approach the food dish.

"Muffin!" Beth exclaimed when she saw him. "There you are. Now to find Ivan."

"Here he is," Kurt was carrying a rather large orange and white stripped cat. "I found him in the laundry room, trying to get behind the washer and dryer, but he's too fat to fit."

"Ahh it's so sad. How could someone just up and drop them off." Beth continued to try and get Buddy to eat. "Muffin seems to be accepting us. But Buddy. There is just something in his eyes, as if he's heartbroken."

"He probably is. Imagine your entire life with someone and then they just dump you. I can't believe after 13 years she simply dumps them off." Kurt said almost exactly what Buddy had said to me. I sat there in shock at hearing the words coming from my master's mouth too.

"And these guys for over ten years. Unbelievable!" Beth replied while still trying to get Buddy to purr, of which he was not going to have any part.

"I just hope they will adapt. They are pretty old. Except for Ivan. He's only two so he might adjust." Kurt was inspecting them as he talked about the new comers.

"I just wonder how anyone could do this." Beth continued attempting to get Buddy to respond but he simply refused and eventually got up and walked away. Beth sat there watching him leave. A feeling of helplessness quickly overtaking Beth's spirit.

Later on that night I heard the whimpers of Buddy and went to see what I could do. I found him in the master bathroom perched on top of a large shelf.

"Don't cry Buddy," I tried to comfort him and moved closer to keep him warm.

"Why doesn't she want me anymore?" he asked over and over again.

I tried to consul him, "I don't know. But you're here now. Please accept that."

In response he simply moved away from me so I moved with him. Eventually after an hour or so, Buddy seemed to calm down and breathe easier. We had just gotten into a deep sleep when Beth came into the room. She seemed to instinctively understand that Buddy was a cat in distress. She picked him up and took him back to bed with her. I watched she used her own blanket to comfort him. In time, they were both breathing deeply so I knew they were asleep. I used the opportunity to jump up and curl next to Kurt who was in deep sleep. I laid there and gazed into his face. My owner loved me, he would never leave me. Suddenly, a dark thought crossed my mind. Of course he would never leave me but I would someday leave him. Why did I suddenly think this? I shook my head back and forth attempting to get the irrational thought out of my head.

"Stop it. Stop it. Stop thinking that," I told myself over and over to the point that my insistent shaking was beginning to wake Kurt. His breathing became less deep and he was beginning to arouse ever so slightly. I stopped and his breathing again deepened. I settled myself on the side of the bed where I could still cuddle up to my precious human, but allow him the room to sleep peacefully. I wanted to stay here forever in his arms, but I knew that eventually it would come to an end. It would be morning, and the hectic pace of life would begin. It always did, and it always would. But for how long for me, was the last thought I had before allowing myself to go into that land of deep sleep. Even Buddy had permitted himself to finally give in and curl up against Beth on the other side of the bed. During the night more cats appeared and slept in various spots on the bed, but this didn't bother the humans. They were used to sharing their bed, and as long as there was love and attention it couldn't be wrong.

<<< TWENTY-EIGHT >>>

The days seemed to blur into each other, most of the days began like exactly the same. The humans would arise to the screeching sound of an alarm. I could never figure out why most days they enjoyed this annoying sound. Then there were those few days when they would sleep, until the natural time rhythm of their body would tell them it was time to wake up. Those were the best days. They would be home for most of the day and attention would be plentiful for us. Once in a while during those rare days, the humans would leave after packing some food in their car and making sure all of the cats were safely in the house. On such days they came home late at night, but we didn't mind because they would be in a very different mood, sometimes smelling of salt water and sand. Those were the days when the owners seemed to be happy and had an attitude of peace about them.

We tried to make them happy too and they did enjoy our company. The four new cats, Buddy, Sasha, Muffin, and Ivan were attempting to adjust. Buddy most days would sit on the bathroom shelf, moving only to use the litter box and get an occasional drink of water. Beth and Kurt had given up trying to get him to feed at the food bowl and had begun bringing him food in a smaller dish and leaving it with him on the shelf. He would occasionally take a few bites but no more than to keep him just surviving. He had begun to lose a noticeable amount of weight and not only the cats noticed but so did the humans. They continued to shower him with perhaps more affection than what they showed the rest of us.

Ivan had taken to hiding in the laundry room and came out to eat only when he was starving. Then he would eat hurriedly so as not to mingle with the rest of the clan. Ivan was antisocial, or so that was what Kurt had referred to him as.

The ragamuffins, Sasha and Muffin seemed to be adapting the best. They often fed at the dish with us and Sasha loved to nibble and play bite, when one of the humans would pet him. They nicknamed him "Bitter" because of the way he would nip and then dash off. Muffin on the other hand was always up to playing red-dot-of-light game, and he had become almost proficient at catching it, which had amazed all of the cats. However, when his paws came up, the red-dot-of-light was gone, causing our owners to roar with laughter, when they saw the puzzled look on his face. If only Buddy would try to accept this wonderful home with all the love he ever needed. If only he would try to accept the love. But it wasn't to be.

One night I heard him talking, so I walked quietly in to listen.

"I see the bridge. I am going there. I want my owner and I know she is there." He kept repeating over and over again.

I was at a loss to understand how a cat could see their owner at the bridge. It was supposed to be the other way around. The owner saw their pet. How could he see the owner? I just had to ask.

"Buddy?" I ventured in. "Are you dreaming?"

"No, Whitie, I don't dream," was the seriously quiet response.

"What bridge are you talking about?" I just had to know.

"The Rainbow Bridge. My owner is there waiting for me." His quiet response broke the silence of the night and also brought Ranger in as well.

"Whitie, don't you know why they were brought here?" Ranger questioned me.

"I assumed it was because their owner didn't want them anymore. Why are we all here? Left by people." Why had I said that? I wondered, even as the words came out of my mouth.

"No, Whitie. His owner passed onto the other side of the Rainbow Bridge. She knew she was dying and she wanted her pets to have a good home before she left. She had no one but her cats, and she loved them so much she wanted them to be taken care of, even when she could barely take care of herself." Ranger was sounding ominous now.

"I saw her. She told me she would wait for me. I'm going there tomorrow." Buddy said with a resolve so strong that I believed him now.

"Buddy, how…I mean…why…oh I don't know about any of this." I was at a loss for words now. Here I am The King and I couldn't even help out an old cat whose owner had died.

"It's the way Buddy wants it," Ranger exclaimed.

That moment a reality dawned on me. Not about Buddy, but Ranger. I determined in my mind that if something ever did happen to me first, I wanted Ranger to take charge. I would deem him The King and he would be a great leader for the clan. I would do this

147

before crossing the Rainbow Bridge. I would grant him the freedom to lead.

We both slept next to Buddy that night, keeping him as comfortable as possible. In the morning when the owners awoke, I saw the look on their faces as they realized Buddy had died.

"Cats know more than we give them credit for," Kurt responded in a tone I had never heard from him before.

Gently Kurt picked up Buddy and they both spent a few moments petting his lifeless body before leaving the room with him in Kurt's arms. I looked at Ranger and we both knew Buddy was at peace now. He was finally with his owner again and the two of them would be playing on the other side of the Rainbow Bridge and they would experience happiness forever.

The mood at the house was somber for the remainder of the day and most of the clan watched out the window as Kurt used the shovel to dig a hole in the backyard and then very gently they wrapped Buddy's body in warm soft blanket for his trip across to the other side. But we all knew he was already there and only his body would be left back here on earth, animals are given a brand new body, free of any pain or other conditions that might plague them. Once on the other side they would only experience love and for that there could be no better place.

<<< TWENTY-NINE >>>

Weeks went by after Buddy's death and the clan appeared to be dealing with the death so I resumed my outside explorations. Of course the house up the street was my place of habit. Oddly enough, the humans seemed to have disappeared leaving almost no sign that they had ever been there. I wasn't at all surprised since several nights ago there was a loud commotion and all the neighbors including Kurt and Beth were outside it the middle of the night. The loud booming noise had scared us all awake, humans and cats both. I looked out the front window from my couch perch, and saw Kurt and Beth standing on the porch while other humans from the neighborhood were much more adventurous, some even walking closer to the house up the street to get a better view. I was reminded of the day of the house fire, when the neighborhood humans stood in the front yard and were curious. I guess humans are curious like cats and will travel to satisfy their curiosity even if it means having to walk somewhere to do so.

I saw several people put into the cars with the lights on them and they walked rather oddly with their hands behind them and glittering rings around their hands. Several men came out of the cars with lights on the top and put yellow tape around the house and yard. I wondered if they were doing that to keep cats away but it didn't matter because I could easily walk under that tape.

Several days later a visitor came to the door and I was reminded of the day when a visitor brought four cats to our house. Only this time instead of cats coming, one was going. I recognized the visitor immediately and brushed up against her anxious to let bygones be bygone. It was Debra, she had come to visit us, I was sure of that.

"Well hello there Whitie," She gushed over me and I was glad to return the favor this time.

For a fleeting moment I flinched back with the thought that perhaps she might take us back to her house but then I realized how ridiculous that was and brushed up against her again. The humans were talking in excited tones so I decided to follow them through the house and eventually we ended up in the laundry room. Ivan's favorite place to hide. Ivan had become more recluse lately making Beth and Kurt even more concerned about him, especially after Buddy had died.

"We've tried everything we can to help him adjust but I think he needs to be an only cat," Beth was talking to Debra and I was unable to make out most of what she was saying. I understood cat and adjust but nothing else made much sense to me.

"I've really missed the cats since they left," Debra was now talking about us.

"He's young, declawed, and litterbox trained. I think he would be great with you." Kurt joined in now. Still I was at a loss to fully understand the deal being made over Ivan. He was a loner and though he had been here long enough to understand and fit in, he refused to. I had even had a stern talk with him one night, but all he did was lay his head down and feign sleep, virtually ignoring me.

"I will try. Not sure it will work," Debra responded.

"If it doesn't work you can always bring him back," Beth reassured Debra. "I would say give him at least a month. It's taken us longer than that and with losing Buddy he seems to be even worse now. I think the change of scenery will help."

Before long, Ivan had been placed in a litter-less box and Debra was carrying it out the door. I realized almost too late that it was the exact same litter-less box he had arrived in. I was even more confused now than ever before.

"Why were my humans allowing Debra to take Ivan with her?" I simply couldn't make sense of it all.

"Whitie, Ivan is unhappy here." Bear suddenly appeared by my side.

"But everyone is happy here," but I knew even as I said that how untrue it was.

"Buddy wasn't," Baby chimed in. I hadn't even seen him come over.

"No, he wasn't. But Ivan gets so much attention," I still tried to make sense of it all. "Perhaps Debra can make Ivan happy," I finally agreed as the door shut taking Ivan away from us.

The rest of the clan seemed to simply accept that Ivan was gone, but I didn't. I intentionally sniffed for the next several days in the two spots his scent was the strongest. I knew my humans were closely observing my actions, but I didn't care. I needed to understand why some cats were abandoned by their owners and other humans were filled with so much love for their cats. I knew Debra would love Ivan in a way that only a chosen human was permitted to love. I had seen the way Ivan cuddled up to her when she went into the laundry room and how he had simply crawled into the litter-less box, content to leave. He hadn't even said goodbye to the rest of the cats.

That was probably the final detail that I knew deep down confirmed that he did not want to be here. He had chosen his human and it wasn't Beth or Kurt. It was Debra. I had hoped she would not put him in the room we had been in, but would allow him free reign of the house. Deep down I knew she would, and with that thought I decided not to bother sniffing out his scent anymore.

<<< THIRTY >>>

Two weeks had passed since the odd happenings at the
adventure house, yet there still were no humans. In a way I was
glad for that fact. The last time I was there and approached by a
human, his movements made me uneasy. He tried to walk toward
me but seemed all out of sorts just trying to walk. I had never seen
a human do that before, except the one time Beth was sick. She
tried to mop the floor, one of the daily chores she and Kurt do, but
when she moved back and forth with the mop she staggered until
finally Kurt came into the kitchen. He took the mop from her, and
ordered her to go to bed. Something he said about her being sick
and the flu. I'm not sure what flu is but I do know what sick is. I
was sick myself and the vomiting that accompanied it was not
pleasurable. Apparently I had eaten something that didn't agree
with me and it for two days I was so sick, that all I wanted to do
was hide behind the bed.

This man was like that except he wasn't vomiting and I couldn't
see anyone telling him to go to bed. Yet, he appeared to be sick but
at the same time, he didn't really seem sick. It was a very odd
experience for me and one in which I had no desire to repeat, so
whenever I would venture there I was extra cautious of avoiding
him. But now there didn't appear to be any humans at all again.
Very similar to the time Hobo, who used to be Kitty-Kitty came to
us. All of the humans were void of this place but it still smelled
slightly reminisce of humans.

This time there was only the odd scent that continued to lure me
closer as I approached the silent house. There it was, a whiff of
something strong smelling even before I was there. I noticed now
there were several plastic containers and the odd smell seemed to
be especially strong coming from the containers. I cautiously
approached them, even though deep down within me, my instincts
told me it could be dangerous, but I didn't care. I simply had to
satisfy my need for exploration and adventure despite my eyes
beginning to water at the intense odor.

Ranger's words of warning came tumbling at me suddenly,
stabbing me with a need to stop in my tracks. I did so only
momentarily, I couldn't allow him to take over my sense of

adventure. All cats needed a good hunt and that was exactly what I was doing. I was hunting down the strange, and in a way, hurting scent. I had to know what it was, I had to investigate, regardless of the outcome. My desire to go back and let Ranger know that I was the one in charge and I was The King was overpowering my primal need to avoid danger. I was in charge of me, not Ranger, or anyone else in the clan. No one could take that away from me, not even Kurt. Ranger might think he would make a great leader, and I couldn't help but believe he would eventually someday, but I would decide when it was time for me to pass down the leadership. Right now was simply not the time.

I was so engrossed in having a one-sided argument with another cat who wasn't even here with me, that I didn't realized I had stumbled upon a broken crate until I dove headfirst through it. Immediately I regretted not paying attention because of the intense burning sensation, which left me feeling as if the breath had been sucked right out of me. I found myself inside the now overturned container, lying at an odd angle and gasping for breath. I listened as the grass around the container made an odd sound, like bacon sizzling and I was too dumbfounded to realize that, I too, was sizzling. What felt like from the inside of my body to my very whiskers.

The realization that I was on fire instantly jolted me into action. I jumped around attempting to escape the awful explosions going on inside my body and then just as I had leaped clear of the container I suddenly felt a tremendous tremor overtake me. I shook until I fell over with my tongue hanging out at an odd sideways angle from my parted lips. I suddenly felt very warm, almost as if I was hanging over a fire and the sweat popped out of my paws, the dripping sensation trying to cool my inner heat. That wasn't working so I began to pant, something cats rarely do expect in extreme heat. I knew it was a nice cool day. So why was I so hot?

In the distance I heard Kurt calling for me. My mind was running as fast as it could to him but my body remained overturned and rigid with all four legs stretched out and violently shaking. I tried to clear my head of the horrible burning scent. The air surrounding me reeked of the putrid stench, similar to the smell of an animal dying. Wait, there was a dead animal. It looked like a small squirrel lying less than a foot from me. He appeared to be distorted, bloated, and burn marks covered his slowly decaying body. The odd part, I realized was that there were no marks from vultures eating at him. It was almost as if the vultures, the same ones who picked Sweetie's body clean of any flesh, weren't interested in this meal.

I could still Kurt calling but then I heard the door shut and his voice was as gone as the squirrel. Slowly, as if on their own accord, my legs released their trembling and I tested if they still had the ability to carry me home. The first attempt was useless so I laid back down again and concentrated on the poor dead squirrel. I wondered what had happened. He appeared, at first, to be swollen full of the nuts they ate. Often preparing themselves for colder months, when none could be found. Squirrels were not as fortunate as cats and had to find their own food. Even more strange, was that his body had an odd scent about it. Perhaps it was the scent that had kept the vultures from enjoying such a fine meal. The more I concentrated on the smells enveloping him, a rising panic began to surface in my own body. This scent, this unique odor was similar to the one from the container I had just fallen into. The grass surrounding the container was also coated with the odd aroma. Then a sheer terror arose from deep within my soul when I suddenly realized I too was coated with this same putrid stench.

Ranger's words of warning came back to me fully now. "My overpowering desire for adventure, for testing the unknown would someday get me." I could almost hear him saying now, as if he were here. Was today the day? No, I had to get back home, back to my human, my chosen one. He would help me. He would take me in his arms, make this horrid feeling go away.

With that thought, I forced myself up on my feet and began what now appeared to be, the longest walk of my life. One step at a time, I would get there. I was tired. I was more than just tired. I was collapsing deep inside of myself. My paws left wet marks on the blades of grass from the sweat that refused to stop pouring out of me. The air came in great gulps, each one tearing into my lungs, with a ferocious ripping, that surely was breaking open my entire body.

Two more yards to trek through, the night was coming on fast. How long had I been out? Time seemed to have no reference for me and I continued on, finally at the bottom of the porch steps. I simply could not make it up there. Instead I used the concrete slab at the bottom of the stairs as a resting spot. At least here someone would see me, in the grass it could be a hit or miss.

I wasn't sure how long I had been there when Beth opened the door and began looking at the street from where I had come from. She peered intently at that house, the one I would never venture to again. No amount of excitement could entice me to repeat that mistake. Hobo was smarter than me when she gave up that dreaded, horrid place.

I tried to raise my head but lacked the strength to do so. Somehow I had to get Beth's attention. I gazed at her out of my half closed eyes and thought perhaps she didn't see me. Surely, she saw me. I had to keep the faith. Just as that thought was beginning to fade away, along with what little resolve I had to continue on, Beth looked at the bottom of the steps and her mouth flew open.

"Whitie!" her scream pierced the night air. "Kurt, come quick. Whitie's hurt!"

No I did not want Kurt to find me. I did want to feel his arms holding me, his gentle stroking of my fur. But not seeing me like this. I knew my human would be upset and that was not being a good cat. I knew.

Kurt came out in a full blown rush. He ran down to the bottom of the steps and gently picked me up.

"I think he's been hit by a car!" Beth continued on in her frenzied voice.

"No, he doesn't appear to have anything broken." Kurt was now running gentle hands over my body. I could still feel his hands but they no longer were comforting, instead every inch that he touched felt oddly on fire. It was almost as if I could barely stand to be touched. My body was not reacting normally and I was unable to control my reactions. Actually, I was not reacting at all. I was simply lying there in Kurt's arms unable to communicate with him that I was still here. I was still his King. I still wanted to ride the food cart and lie in his arms on the soft warm bed. I still wanted to chase the red-dot-of-light, and dig my feet into fresh litter. I wanted to head butt him my kisses and purr when he and I were together. Unfortunately, my body and mind were now two separate entities.

"We need to get him to the vet. There's something wrong."

Kurt began as he carried me in. He put me ever so gently on the table while he and Beth began frantically running around the house. One by one the other cats came and sniffed me over. Bear head butted me some kisses, while Sasha gave me a gentle nip. Sparkles was perplexed at my sudden motionless body and she backed away when my eyes moved. Each of them seemed to instinctively understand what I knew was going to happen. It was just as Ranger had predicted. Oh why didn't I listen to him?

Just then Ranger jumped up and gazed into my eyes. I could read his thoughts and for one last time we communicated what needed to be said.

"Ranger, you were right. My adventurous spirit was too much for even me to handle," I silently told him as only cats can do with their eyes. Humans will never be able to speak with their eyes as cats do.

"Whitie, you are and always will be The King of our clan. I will miss you. Tell the others they are not forgotten when you get there." Ranger wanted his last words to be of encouragement and comfort.

I was too tired and the room was spinning so I simply shut my eyes. Beth recognized that and became hysterical.

"He's dead! He's dead!" I heard her screaming so I forced myself to open my eyes. This was not the way I wanted to end it. I needed Kurt. He was my human. I needed him to comfort me. I knew this was going to be the end. I saw the plastic litter-less box of death being put beside me and I forced myself to rouse. I would not be put in there. I knew what that meant and I would not. I would fight it. I was still The King, and a King decides how he leaves this world. I would not do it in that. No!

Gratefully Kurt understood. He picked me up and wrapped me in a blanket. I hadn't realized my body was now trembling with cold, a deep penetrating cold that could not be helped even with the warmth of my owner's body enveloping me in this soft blanket.

"We don't need that Beth. Leave it! Let's go." Kurt commanded as we rushed out the door and into the car.

Beth was driving and neither one said a word the entire trip. I hung on. I still knew I was going to die but I didn't want to quit yet. I looked into Kurt's eyes and tried to communicate with him in the way only cats can. I wanted him to know that I was his cat, his

King, and that I would wait for him, no matter how long it took. As he gazed down upon me, I felt for a split second that he understood. These humans with their complex lives, somehow could understand the unspoken voice of a cat. But only if the human belonged to the cat. With that I relaxed, closing my eyes and reminisced back on my life. I had met many cats. I had rescued them from a bad life, from bad people, from terrible owners who simply had thrown away their beloved cats as if they were dirty litter. Then I began to regret my adventurous side. I was still young, for a cat, that is. I had so much more living to do. Why hadn't I listened to Ranger? He had tried to warn me.

We got to the vet's office in what seemed like a minute but then I realized I had shut my eyes and fallen into a deep sleep. Beth held the door as Kurt rushed in and took a seat not wanting to let go of me for even a second. I opened my eyes and gave Kurt's hand a slight nudge. I thought at first he hadn't even felt it but then he gently kissed the top of my head, so I knew then he had.

I heard Beth talking in frantic tones to the lady behind the counter but I couldn't make out a word she was saying. I had been here several times in my life. Mostly they were good times when people would dote over me and gush about how gorgeous I was. Of course there was that one time when I was sent home with a plastic cone on my neck and my front claws were gone. However, that time though, both of my sisters were with me and they too had the same cone on their necks.

Gray, I wondered if she would be there waiting for me. I had not thought about Gray for such a long time now. There were even times when I had literally forgotten about her, but now her face was so clear it was almost as if she was right in front of me now.

Beth joined Kurt sitting on the bench beside him and I heard them Beth talking in hushed voices as I tried to make out what they were saying.

"Did you see anything?" Kurt was asking.

"No, he was just lying at the bottom of the steps. I think I saw him earlier at that house. The one the cops were at and arrested all those people for making meth. You don't think…" Beth's voice trailed off.

"I don't know what to think right now. The vet needs to know that's a possibility though," Kurt replied, his voice sounded even more strained than it was at the house.

We sat there for almost an hour. I was losing my resolve to hang on and Kurt sensed this when he barked a command at Beth.

Beth rushed up to the counter, her voice getting louder. I heard the word die and while I knew the fact that I was going to die, the reality of death suddenly hit me. I was dying. I would never ride the food cart again. Never sleep in Kurt's arm. The house would now be ruled by another cat, I hoped Ranger would step up to the plate. I would never again lead the pack out on an adventure. On the other side though, I would be able to play with Gray and Sweetie. I would even see Star. I wondered if he had both eyes now. Would Sweetie convince me to try out the bubble bath? Buddy. I wondered if I would be with Buddy or if he would be somewhere with his owner. Would I see how happy Buddy is? I was sure I would meet up with Buddy again.

I was The King and I was going to cross over the Rainbow Bridge soon. There was a finality in that thought.

"He's sick. We're afraid he might have gotten into some meth or something at a house up the street. NO! We don't do meth. What do we look like? Druggies? It's the idiots up the street." Beth's voice was projecting louder over the large room, which had suddenly become quiet, while the rest of the people, with their pets, turned their attention to Beth. "Will you just get the vet? Our cat is dying! Do you want him to die in the waiting room?"

I turned my face and looked at Kurt for the last time. Tears were streaming down his face and his upper body was heaving as bouts of crying overtook his rigid demeanor. My body was striving to breath but no breath was coming. Beth rushed over at that moment and I turned my head toward my human, my chosen one. I forced myself to head butt him one last time and then a shudder overtook me as my last parting breath left out in a ragged swoosh.

I saw the Rainbow Bridge and Gray standing there waiting with Sweetie as well as all the others awaiting their humans. Mother Cat, whom I had long forgotten about was the first one on the other side. I saw Buddy with his human, the lady who I thought was so cruel suddenly became one in which I saw his delight in. Buddy was happy. I wanted so badly to cross that bridge, but knew my spirit had one more task on this earth to do. I had to give control of the kingdom to Ranger. He was, after all, my comrade, the one who rightfully deserved my position in the clan.

My spirit dove from this side of the Rainbow Bridge down to the house on earth for one last time. My spirit floated to Ranger and as his eyes grew large with recognition I spoke my final words.

"Ranger, you are now The King," I communicated as only cats can do, with such calmness he had no other choice but to accept.

"No Whitie, you will always be The King. But I will ride the food cart for you."

With that final task completed, I permitted myself to join the others, knowing I had adventures to partake in and my never ending thirst for exploration would go on, until such a time that my human would join me. I would wait for him. I prayed it would be a long time, but I would still wait.

Kurt and Beth made a nice place for my body to rest. Partially under the garage in the backyard where I had enjoyed playing a game with Kurt. I would hide under the garage by the big rolling door and then dart at him when he came out. Kurt came to visit me several times during the first couple of weeks. He would sit and talk to me, calling me his King. Other times he would just sit there by the place where my body laid now beginning the decaying process. It was all a part of nature and I was now in my new body but my spirit still had not completely made a home yet on the other side of the bridge. My spirit could sense a deep sadness in Kurt and I also felt his resolve that he knew he and I would be together again when it was his time to meet me on the Rainbow Bridge. I knew he sometimes felt me, as my spirit brushed up against him in the movement of the wind. A slight breeze would make him shutter as he felt me head-butt him, showing my never ending love. But I also knew that I had to make my crossing final. I could not continue to hover between the two realms. My place now was with the others. I would wait and while I was waiting, I would satisfy my thirst for adventures, accompanied by those in my clan who had already made the other side of the Rainbow Bridge their heaven.

I only needed to know that Kurt would be all right. I needed the reassurance that another would commit to him, because all humans need a cat to rescue them from this crazy life. And then one day to Kurt's utter amazement it happened.

One day, while pulling out the food cart, Ranger suddenly jumped up, sitting proudly, and with a chocked voice I heard Kurt say, "Let's go Ranger. Protect me from hostile kitty-cat territory."

ABOUT THE AUTHOR

Mabel Elizabeth (Beth) Livingston has been writing since the young age of eleven. She would often get in trouble as a student for writing, instead of paying attention in class. *Whitie – The Cat Who Rescued Humans,* is Beth's first published novel but not her first published writing. Beth has written for her small town newspaper, wrote and published various newsletters, and informational pamphlets, poetry, and a children's book entitled, *How Many are Too Many?* A children's book that uses the story of her rescued cats to teach preschool and early elementary math skills. She hopes to publish a children's version of Whitie.

Beth is a talented writer and has the ability to create characters with unique personalities. She not only enjoys writing, but loves teaching her students how they can love writing at Mulberry High School, where she is involved in the dual enrollment program. Beth is also an adjunct professor of English at Polk State College.

A graduate of Southern New Hampshire University, Beth received her Master of Fine Arts degree in English and Fiction Writing. She also earned a Master of Arts degree in Education at Warner University. Beth is a member of Sigma Tau Delta, International English Society and Phi Theta Kappa Honor Society.

Beth and her husband Kurt live in the small town of Mulberry, Florida, located between Tampa and Orlando. When she is not writing or teaching, Beth enjoys spending time with her husband Kurt. They enjoy riding motorcycles, going to car shows, and spending time relaxing. Currently she is working on her second novel the sequel to Whitie. Beth is the proud mother of three adult children, Robert, Angelo, and Karrah D'Agostino. She is also the proud Nana to eight grandchildren.

Of course she and her husband run a small rescue and are kept busy with their dogs and cats. You can follow Beth and her cats on her Facebook page at Whitie Cat or her website at
whitiethecatwhorescuedhumans.com

Made in the USA
Lexington, KY
12 June 2018